Susan Hiller : Recall

Published by BALTIC, Gateshead, in association with Museu de Arte
Contemporânea de Serralves, Porto and Kunsthalle Basel on the occasion
of the exhibition *Susan Hiller: Recall Selected Works 1969–2004* at BALTIC.

BALTIC, Gateshead
May 1 – July 18 2004

Museu de Arte Contemporânea de Serralves, Porto
October 15 2004 – January 9 2005

Kunsthalle Basel
January 30 – March 27 2005

Susan Hiller : Recall

Selected Works 1969 – 2004

Edited by James Lingwood

Contents

Acknowledgements

It has been a pleasure to enjoy a close working relationship with Susan Hiller on the exhibition at BALTIC, Gateshead and subsequent presentations of her work at the Museu Serralves in Porto and the Kunsthalle Basel.

Following an initial invitation from Sune Nordgren and Vicki Lewis, several members of the BALTIC team have helped move the project forward over the past year including Pippa Coles, Acting Head of Programme, Nicola Hood, Assistant Curator, Chris Osborne, Technical Manager (Programme), Viv Anderson, John Smith and Stuart Harris, exhibition and A/V technicians respectively, Wendy Lothian, Exhibitions Administrator and Nina Byrne, Media Officer. We are delighted that this exhibition inaugurates the new Directorship of Stephen Snoddy.

Special thanks to the inspired technical team who have contributed so positively to the making of a new work, *Clinic*, in particular Adrian Fogarty. The new work has also benefited greatly from the commitment of David Cunningham, Michelle Hirschhorn, and her assistants Kai Ozawa, Clara Podda, Chiara Sartori, Angelika Tomaszewski who co-ordinated the recording of the testimonies, as well as the staff at BALTIC. We are also indebted to the hundreds of volunteers who 'gave voice' to the accounts of Near Death Experiences for *Clinic*.

The Tate Gallery have been strong supporters of Susan Hiller's work for two decades, and a full presentation of her work would not be possible without their involvement. We would like to thank Sir Nicholas Serota, Director of Tate, Jan Debbaut, Director of Tate Collections, Frances Morris, Senior Curator at Tate Modern, Catherine Kinley, until recently Senior Curator of Tate Collections, Sarah Joyce, Conservator of Electronic Media and Catherine Clement, Senior Loans Registrar for their generous co-operation. Thank you to Isobel Johnstone and Jill Constantine of the Arts Council Collection and to Ryan Rogers of the Hayward Gallery for his technical support. We have also benefited greatly from Robin Klassnik's advice, and from Gabriel Coxhead's assistance at Susan's studio in London.

Susan Hiller's work has stimulated some exceptional writing over recent years. We are privileged that Guy Brett and Jean Fisher have contributed new essays on aspects of her work, and that Rosemary Betterton, Ian Hunt, Louise Milne, Denise Robinson and Stella Santacatterina have reworked essays for this book. Mark Diaper has cared for every aspect of this book's design and production with an exemplary patience and eye for detail.

Following the exhibition at BALTIC, different exhibitions of Susan Hiller's work will be presented at the Museu Serralves in Porto and the Kunsthalle Basel. Many thanks to João Fernandes, Director and Ulrich Loock, Deputy Director of the Museu Serralves and Adam Szymczyk, Director of the Kunsthalle Basel for their generous collaboration on the exhibition and publication. Finally, I would like to thank Susan for her energy and commitment in the planning and realisation of the project.

James Lingwood

Preface

BALTIC are delighted to welcome Susan Hiller back to the North East for her first major exhibition since her tenure as BALTIC Professor of Contemporary Art at the University of Newcastle between 2000 and 2003. *Susan Hiller : Recall – Selected Works 1969–2004* brings together a wide range of work on the Ground Floor and Level 3 at BALTIC and includes a new commission, *Clinic,* in the large Level 4 gallery.

The assigning of Susan Hiller's exhibition to three major galleries at BALTIC reflects the significant contribution the artist has made to the landscape of contemporary art. Renowned for working in a variety of media, the artist has made important video, installation and audio works and continues to push the boundaries of her chosen media and to set new standards for younger generations of artists.

The exhibition foregrounds works which have been brought about with particular regard to collecting and excavating, often based on rejected or ignored aspects of our shared culture. It includes early and ongoing pieces such as *Painting Blocks* (1974–84) and *Measure by Measure* (1973–ongoing) and several major installations including *An Entertainment* (1990), *From the Freud Museum* (1991–97), *Wild Talents* (1997) and *Witness* (2000). In addition BALTIC has commissioned a major new work, *Clinic,* for the Level 4 gallery, a substantial space with 8 metre high ceilings characterised by its quality of natural light. As the publication goes to print, the artist is working on an audio landscape made up of hundreds of recordings of stories recounting Near Death Experiences. The work will make minimal physical alterations to the gallery, yet will create an extraordinary perceptual experience as well as a remarkable document to a subconscious collective experience.

We would like to extend our thanks to Susan Hiller for her commitment to every aspect of the exhibition and for the privilege of working with her on a new commission. We would also like to thank James Lingwood for working closely with Susan Hiller and with BALTIC as curator of the exhibition and editor of this publication.

Stephen Snoddy

1
___

Midnight, Waterloo 1987

8

Introduction

James Lingwood

In her first exhibition at Gallery House in London in 1973, Susan Hiller presented two works; *Transformer*, a floor to ceiling grid structure with delicate tissue paper sections covered with the artist's marks, and *Enquiries*, a slide show of facts collected from a British encyclopedia to reveal culturally partisan presumptions lurking beneath the guise of objectivity. To enquire, and to transform – these have been two recurring leitmotifs of Hiller's practice in the three decades since her first exhibition. In a remarkably consistent way, Hiller has sustained an open-ended enquiry into the elusive nature of our selves, the forces at work in the making and re-making of subjectivity and its potential for transformation. *Recall* follows the lines of this enquiry through the different forms of Hiller's art – vitrines containing displays of boxes and artefacts; frames enclosing 'automatic' drawings on paper and photographs; screens with shifting fields of colours and words; spaces filled with projected images or resonating with a multitude of voices.

The forms of Hiller's work are diverse (and often ground-breaking in their deployment of different materials and their use of new media), but they share a kind of imprint, which derives from her methods and her materials. Hiller's decision in the mid 1960s to discontinue her work as a young anthropologist has, in much of the critical writing about the artist, taken on an almost Damascene significance; the young researcher, fresh from field trips to Central America, no longer willing to uphold the position of a detached observer, and resolving to be "*inside* all my activities".[1] There is no doubting the significance of Hiller's decision to escape the orthodoxies of academic anthropology. It opened up the space for Hiller to think of her work within the more open-ended discourses of art. However, in recalling a range of projects Hiller has realised over the past 30 years, it seems less a case of one form of activity displacing another, and more as if Hiller spent her formative years as an artist working through the disciplines of anthropology. Certainly the successive phases of research – gathering and collecting, comparison and analysis, presentation and display – constitute a connective tissue through works which on the surface appear to be very different.

Denise Robinson has astutely observed that, in Hiller's work, the figure of "the collector shadows the artist".[2] The selection of work in *Recall* foregrounds this aspect of Hiller's work through the presentation of a constellation of different projects based on collections of objects and experiences. Hiller has first gathered together her materials and then radically reconfigured and recontextualized them to offer different forms of encounter to the viewer. Writing in her postscript to her book *After The Freud Museum*, Hiller notes: "I've worked by collecting objects, orchestrating relationships and inventing fluid taxonomies, while not excluding myself from them ...My starting points were artless, worthless artefacts and materials – rubbish, discards, fragments, trivia and reproductions – which seemed to carry an aura of memory and to hint at meaning something."[3] Surveying her output, it appears that

Hiller has never discontinued the field work; she has instead transferred it to a broader, more open terrain and transformed its distancing strategies into modes of intimacy. From second-hand shops around Britain, Hiller accumulated a large collection of postcards of rough seas around Britain, which she re-presented as *Dedicated to the Unknown Artists*, 1972–76 and which explicitly defined the artist's role as curatorial. Through the 1980s she shot extensive Super-8 film footage of Punch and Judy puppet shows in seaside resorts around Britain which she subsequently made into the video installation *An Entertainment*, 1990. Much of the material Hiller has worked with derives from, or relates to the unconscious – to manifestations of powers or forces from the 'other side'. From herself and her friends and through her on-going research into dreams and their representations, she has collected automatic drawings. From movies she has gathered together sequences of children possessed with special powers (*Wild Talents*, 1997 and *Psi Girls*, 1999). From the global confessional of the internet, she has gathered testimonies from people recalling their sightings of inexplicable phenomena: lights in the sky or UFOs (*Witness*, 2000) – or Near Death Experiences (*Clinic*, 2004). In transferring her researches from the otherness of other cultures to the otherness within our own, and within our selves, Hiller works to stake out a fluid, elusive definition of self and society which constantly challenges conventional mappings of the mind.

How does Hiller work with this material, much of it commonly discarded or distrusted? In what manner, and in what form, does she re-present her gatherings? Hiller talks of her approach as "a kind of cherishing of things". In considering statements of people who have seen UFOs or had Near Death Experiences, she regards their recollections as social facts. They exist, they are widespread, they seem to reproduce themselves with little variation in different cultures around the world. Like the kitsch objects, cheap reproductions and tourist knick-knacks she integrates into *From the Freud Museum*, she takes them at face value; and then she asks questions of them – where have they come from, why do they exist, what belief systems do they embody, what might they mean in another context? She looks or listens with an enquiring critical intelligence, but she does not look down. As she has commented, her procedures constitute an alternative take on the modernist dogma of 'truth to materials.'

During Hiller's years of study in the US, the high priest of post-war Modernism Clement Greenberg was urging that modern art be purged of the 'plague of content.' By renouncing any alien traces or influences Greenberg encouraged artists to aspire to the pure, essential expression of a medium. So painting must be free of the influence of sculpture, both painting and sculpture from theatre etc (let alone dubious materials taken from everyday life). The work must refer to nothing beyond the very conditions of the medium. Hiller's projects from the 1970s onwards mark a return of the repressed. 'Content' – impure, anxious, embedded with a range of associations Greenberg would have regarded as irredeemably corrupting – fills Hiller's work. Rather than the 'no before and no after' of High Modernism, her work overflows with the before and the after. In building the innovative forms of her projects, Hiller achieves a delicate balance which allows this material a double (but never duplicitous) life. It remains true to itself and at the same time becomes something else. Recalled in a new context, it becomes part of a new form, a work by Susan Hiller, and at the same time keeps its identity as part of some other story.

Hiller's renunciation of the classical distance between maker and observer within conventional anthropology was followed by a second renunciation – this time of the status and practice of painting. In the early 1970s, recently relocated to London, Hiller burned or cut up her paintings (an act of unmaking also undertaken by artists in the US such as Lee Krasner, John Baldessari and Gordon Matta Clark). She dispassionately presented (some time later) the evidence of these actions as a kind of memorial archive: storing the ashes of previously exhibited paintings, one for each year of her career since 1973, in long glass burettes (*Measure by Measure*), or cutting up her canvasses and reconstituting them as minimal-like forms (*Painting Blocks*, 1974–84).

From the fissures opened up by this destruction of flatness, a space was opened up for Hiller to explore depth – to go deep into culture and the self and the fundamental issue of how they are formed. Initially, this project led Hiller to make real-time events such as *Dream Mapping* with small groups of friends, and to explore automatic drawing or writing, 'utterances' issuing from a pre-conscious or sub-conscious self. But Hiller has also since the early 1980s used a range of sound and image technologies to push this desire to be 'inside' into more immersive environments. Sound – or more precisely the human voice – is a primary tool in this operation; the voices of the living (for example in the video installation *Belshazzar's Feast*, the sound of the artist's son Gabriel), the voices of the dead (via Konstantin Raudive's scratchy recordings purporting to capture the voices of the dead, which Hiller has used in a number of projects including *Magic Lantern*), or the voices of the living recalling, in her new installation *Clinic* what they experienced when they believed they had died.

Whether realised as museum-like displays or as more encompassing environments, Hiller's projects are marked by a sophisticated understanding of the dynamics of how the visitor encounters and enters the work. She builds a form for the material which both opens a space for critical enquiry and creates an accumulative experience which develops in time. On several occasions, the final form of the work has a direct relationship with the form of the originating material. For example, in the video installation *An Entertainment*, it is as if the puppeteer's box has been exploded into the four walls of the gallery so the viewer is no longer in front of the Punch and Judy show but surrounded and assaulted by it on all sides. *From the Freud Museum* uses a museological vitrine presentation to suggest that "we inhabit an historically-specific museum of culture which might as well be named 'the Freud Museum.'"[3] Similarly, the shape of the forest of speakers in *Witness* relates to the single speaker unit, with its connotations of both UFOs and cruciforms.

Committed though she is to her material, Hiller's subject is not ultimately the objects or the stories but subjectivity itself. Combining intellect and intuition, Hiller's work constitutes an ongoing enquiry into the shifting topology of the self, the fluid forms and elusive edges of identity. What produces the experiences we have, what builds that sense of who we are or who we might be? There are no satisfying Cartesian oppositions in Hiller's work, no clear divide between dream and reality, reason and unreason, individual and collective, feminine and masculine. Through the forms of her art, she delves deep into the dissolution of duality and offers brilliantly resolved works which resonate with unresolvable questions. "May not the prime motive of any work be the wish to give rise to discussion, if only between the mind and itself," Paul Valéry suggested. Ultimately it is the space between the mind and itself which Hiller has so richly explored in her work.

Susan Hiller's Painted Works

Rosemary Betterton

2
___
Susan Hiller at Matt's Gallery, London
Work in Progress 1980

Susan Hiller's Painted Works:
bodies, aesthetics and feminism

Rosemary Betterton

It may seem perverse to base an argument about Susan Hiller's aesthetic strategies on her paintings as she is best known for her major works in new media, video and installation, but it is to her transformation of the practices of painting, and to the embodied subject of aesthetics, that I want to attend. It was the encounter with Minimalism and Conceptual Art in the late 1960s which Hiller drew on to develop a new language through which to make her work. Between 1969 and 1974 she engaged in a variety of artistic activities including performance, group events and recycled works that became the basis for her subsequent practice. This was also the historical moment when a critique of Modernist painting developed alongside an emergent feminist art practice. Hiller's shift from painting to sculpture and the use of found objects can be located within an obscured history of the transition from late Modernist painting to different forms of embodied and material practices undertaken by women artists in the late 1960s. Hiller's early work can be linked with that of another artist, Eva Hesse, who made a similar transition at the time, but whom is usually perceived as belonging to a different generation. I want to revisit that moment in which, for both artists, the categories of gender and painting were beginning to unravel.[1]

I will paint against *every rule I or others have invisibly placed. Oh, how they penetrate throughout and all over.*[2] EVA HESSE

The American critic Rosalind Krauss has described Eva Hesse's wall piece, *Hang Up* (1966) as 'an enormous, empty picture frame, the site of a painting declared and defied at the same time'. Krauss takes this work to be evidence of a refusal, or an inability by Hesse entirely to abandon painting for sculpture. She suggests further that Hesse's work represents the 'optical unconscious' of painting, that which had been repressed within modernism, but continued to trouble, disturb and foul up its logic. Unlike the 'topology of self-containment' offered by a modernist painting, it describes an 'unformed body without organs', dispersed, provoking anxiety, potentially chaotic and threatening to the rational, unified self.[3] Krauss takes Hesse's piece to be representative of a significant moment, not only for Hesse herself, but for Modernism, a point at which its rules were literally turned inside out, and one which marked the beginning of the end for painting. The feminist critic Lucy Lippard also identified *Hang Up* as a turning point, but she saw it as the beginning of something else – the prefiguring of the aesthetic concerns of feminist art practices in the 1970s. What is at stake in these different accounts of endings and beginnings that *Hang Up* represents?

What Eva Hesse said about her work was this: *It is a frame ostensibly and it sits on the wall with a very thin, strong, but easily bent rod that comes out of it. The frame is all cord and rope. It's all tied up like a hospital bandage – as if someone broke an arm... It is coming out of this frame – something and yet nothing and – oh! more absurdity – it's very, very finely done. The colours on the frame were carefully gradated from light to dark – the whole thing is ludicrous. It is the most ridiculous structure that I ever made and that is why it is really good.*[4]

So, for Hesse herself, *Hang Up* was absurd, it corresponded to her desire to make work that was 'something and yet nothing', and yet it was meticulously made, framing and un-framing space with the utmost precision of coloured line.[5] Her ambivalence about the piece is suggested in its punning title: it is both literally hung up on the wall and witness to her own continuing 'hang up' about painting. My own response to *Hang Up* is that, rather than provoking anxiety, it makes me want to step into the empty space – the eight to ten feet – released by the frame. These two elements, the use of a precise absurdity, which mimics yet subverts the rules of painting and the (unspoken) invitation to enter into the space of the work, suggest nothing less than a seismic shift in the aesthetic grounds of abstract art. If, in Jacques Derrida's terms, the function of the picture frame is to maintain the 'conceptual schema' that distinguish form from matter, art from non-art, then here the logic of the frame is disrupted: it is a frame that defines bounded space and yet has itself become the 'body' of the work. The work of Eva Hesse literally opened up the multiple associations of fleshly embodiment that haunted abstract painting to admit the female body with all its connotations of temporality, materiality and excess: 'In a period when cleanliness and straight edges were close to the godliness of success, Hesse... associated concreteness with touch.'[6]

In a series of works called *Painting Blocks* begun in 1970/71 and completed in 1984, Susan Hiller cut up her own earlier paintings and remade them as ten sewn blocks. While Hiller's work is conceptual in its use of series and a Minimalist aesthetic, it has a strong material presence. It returns painting to one of its basic premises as a 'nomad art' made of portable sewn cloth or paper.[7] Neither painting nor sculpture in any conventional sense, the rough and frayed bundles retain certain characteristics of paint on canvas, but appear to be more like three dimensional stitched 'books', with the dimensions of the original painting and dates printed on their covers. While the transformation from painting to block implies a diminution of scale, in this process, the surface becomes a mass, which retains the dimensions of the original. Hiller has commented of these works: *By moving my own works into another state of being, I allow them to participate in life, instead of curating the work as though it were entombed in a museum. There is also a hidden psycho-political agenda: these works express my interest, at a very deep level, in the tactile quality of vision, in 'touching with the eyes'.*[8]

So, what is invested in this transformation from painting to block, from looking to touching, and from tomb to archive? What relationships of paint and touch, space and spectatorship, memory and loss, are mobilised to engage the viewer by non-figurative means?

My desire to 'see' *Painting Blocks* as paintings is frustrated, because the painted surface of the canvas remains hidden. However much I try and catch a glimpse of their coloured interiors, I can only recover their meaning *as* paintings through the tactile qualities of the rough fraying canvas and the date and dimensions given in stark print on the surface of each block. As a viewer, I am engaged in deciphering the relations between the visual and the tactile in which ideas of duration and 'touching with the eyes' are made explicit. This kind of viewing is neither disinterested nor instantaneous, but is directly dependent upon the embodiment of the viewer.[9] *Painting Blocks* evoke an affective response that is situated in the reciprocal relations between vision and touch. And, if the work is seen not only as an *object*, but as part of an intersubjective 'event' that needs a viewer who can move in space rather than a disembodied eye to complete it, then it signifies a more complex relationship involving two beings. The art theorist W.J.T. Mitchell has suggested that pictures face us as subjects that confirm our presence: 'Pictures are things that have been marked with all the stigmata of personhood: they exhibit both physical and virtual bodies; they speak to us, sometimes literally, sometimes figuratively. They present, not just a surface, but a *face* that faces the beholder.' [10] But such 'faciality' is in danger of remaking works of art in human form and such anthropomorphism ignores precisely how, as material objects, they interact with the viewer. More helpfully, Jean Fisher comments that *Painting Blocks* involve: *an experience of* making *or* duration, *encompassing the act of viewing that reinstates a more interactive relation between art and the body…Its process is transformative; not loss of matter, but a change from one state of existence to another.* [11]

The subject-object relation established between the embodied spectator and *Painting Blocks* involves an active process of decoding that not only requires the viewer to mobilise the senses of sight and touch, but to engage with how the work re-configures these senses in a new set of relationships. In ceasing to be paintings, the 'blocks' perform as objects – and such materialisations take time. The change from painting into block, from surface to thickness, and from vision to touch, requires the viewer to engage with the process of *remembering* what looking at a painting is like. It actively reinstates the experience of seeing over time that was disavowed within late Modernist abstraction. Rather than only 'touching with the eyes', I arrive at seeing through a sense of touch, in what has become a complex set of relations between time, space, embodiment and memory.

In so doing, Hiller returns painting to something nearer its performative functions in pre-Renaissance and indigenous cultures, where it acts as a part of ritual, as a talisman or as a manual, conceived as being impermanent yet as having a presence and material effects in the world. [12] This ritualistic element in Hiller's work is evident in another recycled series, *Hand Grenades*, remade between 1969 and 1972, in which she set fire to previous paintings and kept their ashes in glass chemical containers as 'burnt relics'. [13] The transparent glass receptacles imply fragility and the hand-written labels, bearing the title and date of the former paintings, suggest impermanence and non-fixity: 'Like traces and remnants, they point forwards and backwards at the same time'. [14] For if the ashes suggest mortality, the title of the work, *Hand Grenades*, also implies a violent rebirth: these glass memorials have explosive potential. Like the act of cutting up her canvases, Hiller enacts a violent material transformation on her paintings that also enacts a new moment of becoming.

Yves-Alain Bois has associated modern painting with the task of mourning, but suggests that this mourning need not be morbid once we believe in our ability to act in history: 'the desire for painting remains…this desire is the sole factor of a future possibility of painting, that is, of a non-pathological mourning.' [15] But, if painting is a form of mourning, what is 'it' that is being mourned? Making painting, like writing, is a form of making that is also a transformative process. The crossed out word, the layering and repetition of brushstrokes always bears within it a material trace of the past that it effaces. By recycling her paintings, Hiller allows her work to make a transition from entombment to 'another state of being'. She refuses to mourn their passing and, instead, implies that such 'remaindered' work can act as part of a new history. *Measure by Measure*, 1973–ongoing, indeed arose from an accident as a result of which she burned a large canvas and placed it in a glass measuring burette labelled with the title and date of the original painting. This began a process that was repeated annually over the next thirty years that, according to Hiller, 'has to do with measuring time – a contradiction in terms'.[16] A similar contradiction in terms between absence and presence, again staged as a transformation over time, occurred in her project *Work in Progress*, 1980, in which she unravelled canvases and re-worked them into new thread drawings. In these works 'painting' is capable of change and renewal rather than mere repetition or mirroring. Hiller's transformative practice does not offer consolation for loss, but enacts renewal through a practice of making and unmaking, remaking and reparation.

Hiller has referred to retrospective memory as a 'transaction', not a simulation. By this I understand her to mean that her work of investigating and archiving cultural memory involves an active process of exchange with the past rather than a representation of it. Her 'archive' is an index of 'misunderstandings and ambivalences' that have emotional resonance in the present.[17] In works like *Dedicated to the Unknown Artists*, 1972–76, a collection of seaside postcards of 'Rough Sea', and *Fragments*, 1978, based on shards of Pueblo pottery, she invents taxonomies for found objects, which combine rigorous formal ordering with a sense of openness and flux. These works anticipate the much larger ongoing project *From the Freud Museum*, begun in 1992, in which she uses archaeological collecting boxes as 'frames' for various found objects and representations such as divining rods, talismans, photographs or occult texts. These invite viewers to be active participants; like analysts or detectives we search for clues to decipher meanings and events. The connection Hiller makes between psychoanalysis as the investigation of the unconscious and archaeology as an investigation of the past is not fortuitous. Both offer a rigorous 'scientific' method for analysing the hidden and the buried.

These concerns are made explicit in the wide range of Hiller's work that combine painting or drawing with automatic writing in order to explore the marginalised speech of women. In *The Sisters of Menon*, Hiller drew on an earlier project using automatic experiments, somewhere between writing and drawing that she had undertaken in France in 1972.[18] She subsequently lost the manuscripts until 1979, when she made a new work by putting them together in a cruciform layout of four L-shaped panels with additional 'translated' type-written texts. The modular form of the work relates to the open-ended nature of the conversation between the barely articulated utterances of 'women' who are heard through the following text:

who is this one / I am this one / Menon is (1)
Menon is this one / you are this one (2)
I am the sister of Menon / I am your sister / the sister of everyone's sister / I am Menon's sister (3)
I live in water / I live on the air (4)

Menon can be transcribed as 'no men', but also as *nomen* or name.[19] Hiller seeks a language to describe the self, or these multiply imagined selves, without resorting to the individual voice or celebrating an imaginary feminine Other. The voices encompass a range of speakers that cannot be resolved into a singular identity. In the multiple voices of the

Sisters of Menon – 'I', 'you' 'sister', 'everyone's sister' – there is no separation between the subject or object of speech, but rather a refusal of the fixity of self embedded in western ontologies. And, unlike paint on canvas, which acts as a skin that binds the surface, the hand-written and typed texts are more open and porous, without closure or resolution.[20] They enable a viewer to move in and out of the work and to take up other positions, even perhaps to lose her own sense of boundaries: '*My "self" is a locus for thoughts, feelings, sensations, but not an impermeable, corporeal boundary.* I AM NOT A CONTAINER… *Identity is a collaboration. The self is multiple.*'[21]

Hiller's statement resonates with strikingly similar comments on female subjectivity and embodiment in contemporary feminist philosophy.[22] For example, Christine Battersby proposes a model of '"Self"… capable of interpenetration by "otherness"'. She suggests that we need to imagine different metaphors for identity that would describe the specificity of women in new terms: *We need to think individuality differently, allowing for the potentiality for otherness to exist within it as well as alongside it. We need to theorise agency in terms of potentiality and flow. Our body-boundaries do not contain the self; they are the embodied self.*[23]

Hiller's work participates in an ontology in which selfhood is not singular but constructed with otherness – as articulated by Battersby – just as Eva Hesse broke down the boundaries between self and object in her work.

I imagine an encounter between Eva Hesse and Susan Hiller, perhaps at La Guardia Airport in September 1965, Eva returning from Germany to New York via London, Susan leaving for Europe and further East. I think of the conversation that they might have had about beginnings and endings, memory and the future, the death of their mothers, loss and hope, paint and latex, string and thread, performance, art and women's coming liberation…

One of the recurrent themes in the work that I have described here is that of the temporal process of making, unmaking and remaking that remains deictically in the object itself: Eva Hesse compulsively binding her frame like a broken limb; Susan Hiller destroying and remaking her paintings over again.[24] But if we see this 'remaindering' as a refusal to mourn the past so as to give it renewed agency in the present, then a key difference between Hesse's and Hiller's historical positioning as women artists becomes apparent. They are of the same generation, born in 1936 and 1940 respectively, but whereas Hesse, isolated within the male dominated and conventionally gendered avant-garde circles of New York in the sixties, could only enact a refusal of painting and make it 'something and yet nothing' Hiller, working as an artist within an emergent women's movement was able to recast her painting in new terms, to make 'blankness' speak. Hesse was well aware of the multiple ways in which femininity inscribed her role: 'Woman, beautiful, artist, wife, housekeeper, cook, saleslady all these things. I cannot even be myself, nor know what I am',[25] but she had no political language through which to articulate her position. Had she lived, she might, like Hiller, have made the engagement between her practice of art and women's politics.[26] In both cases, their work has played a formative role within the feminist critique of Modernist painting. The work of both Hesse and Hiller shows the complex relations between the material and the semiotic, time and the object, and the psychic and the somatic, that were beginning to be articulated within art around the turn of the 1970s. There is a need to remember the complexities of that historical moment in proto-feminist art before it is either forgotten or mythologised as a state of pre-lapsarian theoretical innocence.[27]

In this essay I have described a practice and aesthetic of making art that differs from the late Modernist claim of 'no before and no after'. The procedures involved in making these works anchor them as physical matter that occupies space and with which we become acquainted through the somatic senses of sight and touch. They are produced both as abstract and material practices that are dependent on a psychic and physical embodiment shared by the artist and her viewers. They can be perceived as enacted through time and as always necessarily incomplete – in the sense that the works continue to alter physically – and as their meanings change. Hesse recognised the fragility and physical degradation of her latex works over time in a nihilistic comment: 'Life doesn't last; art doesn't last, it doesn't matter.'[28] This resonates with Hiller's later, but more optimistic statement: 'In remaking my old paintings I wanted change, but everything changes inevitably...in other societies... sculpture is left to rot...We're different; we think if we can't keep a painting perfect, we'll have no more painting in future.'[29] The death (and life) of painting is recognised and accepted in both these statements as part of the very process of making new art. Both artists have consciously used ritual and repetition, wrapping, binding, layering, folding, in ways that recall the domestic and feminine rituals, as well as some of the fears and doubts that these may hold at bay. And, while such practices have no intrinsic relationship to re-imagining the female subject, by re-embodying vision in a set of intersubjective relationships, they can lend themselves to the representation of different topologies of self. These topologies do not image the female body directly, but evoke it through material traces, voices, and actions, which re-inscribe the body – with difference.

Measure by Measure

1973– ongoing

Painting Blocks 1974–1984

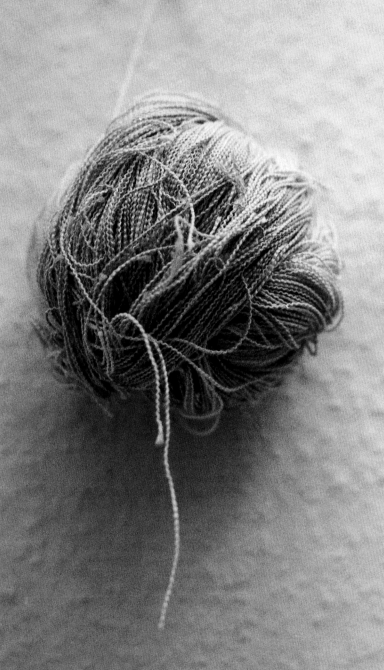

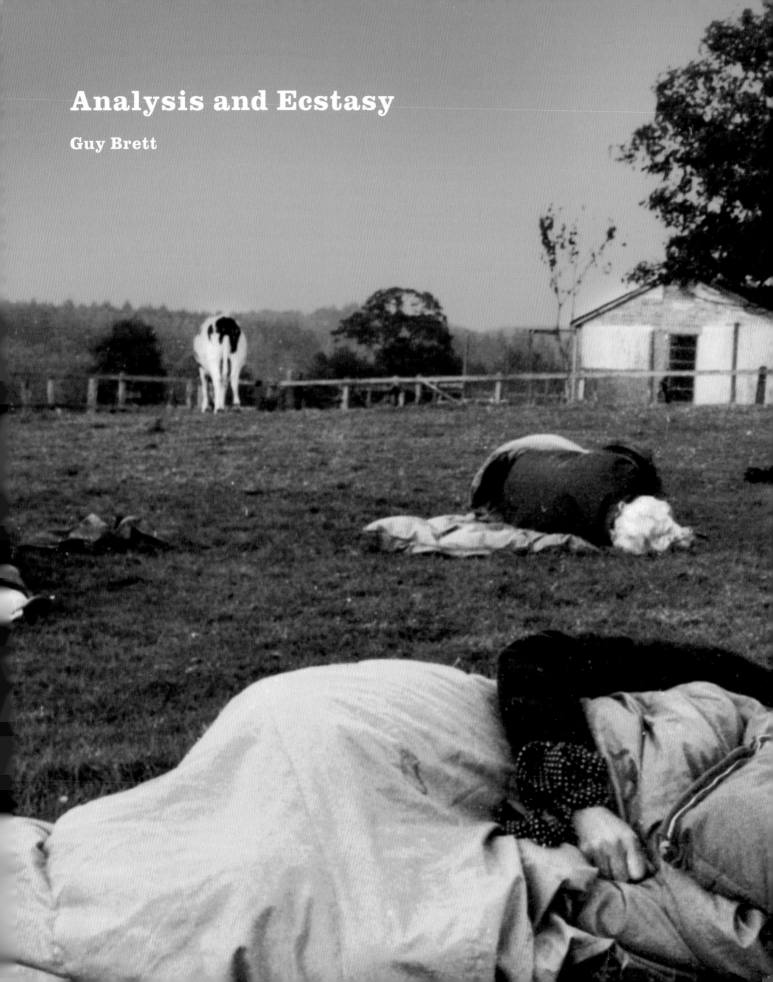

Analysis and Ecstasy

Guy Brett

Dream Mapping 1974
ICA, London 1986

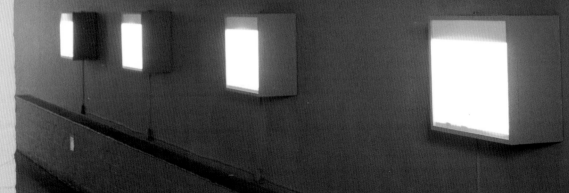

Analysis and Ecstasy

Guy Brett

The group of works by Susan Hiller on which this essay is based have become 'early', when once they were 'current'. The moments at which they were produced have become history, when once they were lived experience. It is now impossible to see them except in relation to what her work became later, just as it is impossible to recapture the impact they had when they first appeared. Hiller's subject matter has changed constantly and her mise-en-scène has been full of surprises and technical innovation, yet her method – her custom of taking some cultural artefact as the starting-point of a passionate quest – has been extraordinarily consistent over the years. In her 'anthology' shows she has been so successful in combining and recombining work of different periods in thematic clusters that all look in a way simultaneous and contemporary. There is an intriguing paradox here. Her works of the 1970s do carry 'signs of the times': for example the idea of organising a collective, mushroom-enhanced, 'dream-in' (*Dream Mapping*, 1974), or of subverting complacent hierarchies of art genres and notions of authorship (*Dedicated to the Unknown Artists*, 1972–76). And yet these works look in no way dated. Perhaps this is because of the sophisticated formal and conceptual structures in which Hiller has re-presented her found materials, making the relationship of earlier to later work intimate and fascinating.

One of the effects of looking back from the vantage-point of today at the group of works I am considering here is to notice how strongly marked they are by the dual training Susan Hiller received: in science (anthropology) and in art (more specifically painting). Her scepticism about the objectivity of science ("I didn't believe there was anything called 'objective truth', and I didn't want to be anything but a participant in my own experience, I didn't want to stand outside it."[1]) led her to abandon anthropology in favour of art. Yet she retained the procedures of systematic research: collecting, classifying, sorting, tabulating, mapping. In turn she became sceptical of the value-laden hierarchy of forms in art (with painting and sculpture placed at the top). Nevertheless her work of the mid 1970s to early 1980s is made in constant reference to the practices of painting, drawing, writing, and sculpture. And although she may have ceased to *be* an anthropologist in becoming an artist, she would play with the traditions and conventions of both, taking both outside their usual frame of reference and even allowing the procedures of each one to interfere mischievously with the other.

Hiller sees a formal origin of her work in Minimalism, and indeed Minimalism's visual and structural aspects, such as the rejection of 'composition' in favour of serial or grid arrangements of the components of a work, tally with those of scientific enquiry. At the same time areas of her interest, and some aspects of method gravitate to an apparently opposite pole, being in key with the Surrealist stream in art and thought: the recurring reference to the dream, suppressed emotion, 'irrational' phenomena, and the technique of automatic writing. The originality of her practice is to work between these supposed oppositions and reconcile them in ways which seem of great importance for our future.

9 [CHAPTER TITLE PAGE]

Dream Mapping
Purdies Farm, Hartney/Whitney,
Hampshire 1974

Dream
Mapping.
P. 46
Thinking Art

In a work like *Dream Mapping* all these impulses are at play. *Dream Mapping* evolved from the earlier *Dream Seminar* and consisted in inviting a number of people to sleep for three nights inside 'fairy rings' of the marasmius mushroom in a certain field in Hampshire. The following days they would draw maps of their dreams in a notebook and as a finale all the individual dream maps would be superimposed on one another, to test the notion of dream 'incubation', and the possibility of "shared structures that underlie individual dreams".[2] The work has usually been displayed as a number of dream notebooks in internally-lit niches in the wall with some of the dream maps re-drawn on a huge scale on the same wall and even ceiling. On the 'science' side, there was the provocation or conceit of applying methodical research strictures to the activity of dreaming ("My work, although contesting the whole notion of the rational and objective, had the look of the rational", she wrote about this period in general).[3] She applied planimetric mapping, diagrammation and notation to the weird space-time and disjointed narrative of the dream, a procedure very different to the Surrealists who made incongruous hybrids and discontinuities from the Western painting tradition. On the 'art' side, she approached the dream world with Minimalism's complete negation of the fantastic. But of course, even super-rational structures like the grid are not without their other side: the grids of cabalistic and numerological lore are supposed to have occult or magical powers.

In terms of art's conventions, *Dream Mapping* took place outside the social and conceptual parameters of the art gallery context of the time. The material resulting from *Dream Mapping* was only presented in exhibition form 12 years after the event. It represented a break (which felt more startling then than it would now) with the assumption of the individually authored art work. Proposed instead was a collective endeavour by anonymous people, initiated but not controlled by the artist and valuing tentative, incomplete, experimental marks more than skill and resolution. John Sharkey wrote at the time: *"The artist is a participator, as well as an originator, of all her projects. Once the overall form has been set and the guide-lines laid out in terms of information data, numbers and kinds of participants, situation or location, etc., she is happy to move into the background and as participant take part in the realisation of the work."*[4]

A dash of irony gave a certain grace and intellectual liberty to the proceedings. Hiller was not a New Age devotee, nor a scientist subjecting a lunatic-fringe phenomenon to rationalist ridicule, but an artist using metaphor to gain insight into certain enigmas of art and life.

But parallel to such works were others that met the prevailing conditions head-on. Hiller continued to paint and subjected her existing paintings to radical deconstructions and transformations. They were cut up into squares and re-sewn together in random order to make new canvasses, or they were cut, tied together in bundles and exhibited on small individual shelves (*Painting Blocks*, 1974–84), they were burned and their ashes displayed in bottles tagged with their original names and collectively re-titled *Hand Grenades* (1969–72), or their threads were unpicked one by one by the artist in public and then re-suspended as skeins and knotted masses about the walls (*Work in Progress*, 1980). Crucially, Hiller maintained that these objects were "as interesting to look at and experience as paintings"[5]. They *were* paintings in a sense. Still tagged with the memory of a great tradition, they showed the folly of a fetishisation of a material or art form as such. Paintings were just a part of everything else.

At the same time the work was propelled by another sort of energy which would sweep through all the traditions of discourse which Hiller had been teasing and testing for possibilities of intellectual liberty and 'truth-telling'. This was the upsurge of the women's liberation movement in the 1970s. Feminism has been through complex changes and intricate debates in the decades since, but the point here is to recall the force, then, of a vast collective undertaking which had the potential to change the world. The growth of feminism generated a completely new orientation on history and intellectual culture. Susan Hiller identified strongly with the movement while maintaining a critical independence within it. What strikes one today in her work and statements of the 1970s and early 80s is her determination to reject impoverished and reductionist categories like 'feminist art' and to link up the feminist with other forms of cultural critique to achieve the "widest possible social implications".[6] The male/female divide would seem to take its place as part of her interest in the reconciliation, mingling and dialogue between dichotomous entities of all kinds in the pursuit of a freer and wider form of knowledge. The 'widest possible implications' are not only social but also cosmological. Whether overt or not, indeed often introduced with subtlety of metaphor, in Susan Hiller's work there is almost always a reference to the elemental force-fields, the vastness of space and time, in which human culture has evolved.

One section of Hiller's key work *Sisters of Menon* (1972–79) contains a diagram in the form of a cross. The left hand side is labelled "MALE" and the right, "FEMALE". On the left side above the cross bar is written "scientists" and equivalent to it on the female side is "mediums". Below the cross bar is written "poets and artists" on the male side and "lunatics and patients" on the female. The art/science divide which Hiller conjured with as a result of her early formation is here subordinated to the male/female divide. 'Mediums, lunatics and patients' represent the categories to which those parts of the scientific and artistic impulse that could not be contained in the patriarchal view of culture were relegated. *Sisters of Menon* contests this relegation as evidence of a monolithic idea of the self, and proposes a "new starting-point. Identity is a collaboration, the self is multiple".[7]

Within Hiller's museum-scale installation, *Fragments* (1978), is a section titled (with a clear echo, and reversal, of Duchampian procedures): "Thirteen Male Absences". The hundreds of pieces of broken pottery of which the work overwhelmingly consists – made by Pueblo women potters and retrieved by the artist from a community rubbish mound – are interrupted by thirteen pieces of flint, the debris left over after projectile point-making, spearheads and arrowheads. Hiller commented: "The male was signified by the absence of his artefacts. It seemed to me important to present that as a kind of alternative picture to the way we usually see things, the female absent from culture".[8] There is another male absence in the piece too: it is inferred by a photograph, taken from National Geographic magazine, of a woman sorting small potsherds. The caption reads: "Patiently Mrs ... puts together jigsaw puzzle fragments ... from the archaeological expedition ... her husbands leads".

These specific references to male absence are swept up into the material presence of the work itself which superbly undermines a monumental, patriarchal domination of the spatial field. The mise-en-scène of *Fragments* made an unforgettable impression on me when I first saw it at Oxford's Museum of Modern Art in 1978. Hiller has called it "a reconciliation of painting and sculpture".[9] 100 small broken pieces of Pueblo pottery were placed on 100 sheets of sketchbook paper laid on the floor in a grid formation. Each sheet also contained a gouache painting of a pottery fragment, different from the actual one resting on the paper.

On the walls were further tiny gouache paintings, more fragments in transparent bags, a photograph and various forms of written statement. The ordering effect of the grid, the bags, the pages, the tabulations, played against the inconclusiveness of the small pieces and their patterns – an inconclusiveness which, however, suggested some larger imaginative reality of which these were indications or tokens. Not-knowing becomes a form of knowing, as Hiller has so often said. The larger reality existed half in dream inspiration, half in waking life, as the many recorded statements of the women Pueblo potters attest.

In *Fragments* Hiller delicately unravels archaeological and anthropological methods to move beyond the primitivist mind-set which sees other cultures as a source of exotic commodities. At the same time she proposes the model of a practice which shows women as 'primary makers of meaning'.[10] *Fragments* was a pioneering work in both senses. Its dispersed space hints at the possibility of a kind of non-exploitative continuum between cultures where common dilemmas can be examined. Its specific cultural references are set within a larger metaphor of experience and thought as fragmentary: "A fragmentary view is all we have".[11] And yet the fragments drive a cycle of creativity. Pueblo potters take inspiration from discarded shards, combing these memory traces of tradition with the utter originality of each individual's dream.

One of the resources which Susan Hiller discovered in aspects of feminist theory was the linking up of the 'analytic' and the 'ecstatic'. She saw this as a confirmation in theory of the experiments she had already been making in her art.[12] No doubt this congruence also felt like a confirmation of her view of art as a "first-order practice, as important as sociology, psychology, physics, politics, or whatever".[13] The congruence of analysis and ecstasy would surely be seen as part of the wider concept of knowing to which feminism, along with other currents of thinking, contributed. In *Dream Mapping* and *Fragments* these two abstract categories are interwoven intricately.

There was surely a further movement at work here: to question the exclusive cultivation of the eye as the privileged means to knowledge, its separation from the other senses, the body as a whole. To question the pre-eminence of the eye was to question the Greenbergian orthodoxy of modernist painting in the 1960s, as Hiller had already been doing in a number of ways. In one of the texts collected in the book *One Way Street*, Walter Benjamin wrote: "*The exclusive emphasis on an optical connection to the universe, to which astronomy very quickly led, contained a portent of what was to come. The ancients' intercourse with the cosmos had been different: the ecstatic trance. For it is in this experience alone that we gain certain knowledge of what is nearest to us and what is remotest to us, and never of one without the other. This means, however, that man can be in ecstatic contact with the cosmos only communally. It is the dangerous assumption of modern men to regard this experience as unimportant and avoidable, and to consign it to the individual as the poetic rapture of starry nights. It is not ...*"[14]

In Hiller's œuvre, the body of works most obviously concerned with 'trance' are those that make use of automatic writing. This group ranges from presentation of Hiller's own experiments in automatic writing (which begins with *Sisters of Menon*), to the abstract calligraphy which this writing eventually developed into, "crypto-linguistic ... , referring to language or pretending to be language ... a set of marks that simply flows"[15] (the photomat works, *Elan*, etc), to works collecting and 'curating' the automatic writing of others (*From India to the Planet Mars*, 1997–2004). The formats vary too: the smaller automatic writing pieces (*Mary Essene, My Dearest, Get William, So Don't Let it Frighten*) are eccentrically framed to echo the scraps of paper they contain and hung in clusters. *From India to the Planet Mars* is a group of light boxes with the script illuminated in white on a black ground. These works usually contain analytic alongside the ecstatic material: in *Sisters of Menon*, for example, small typewritten panels representing the artist's notes and reflections are set at the ends of the cross made up of the sheets of automatic scrawl, the whole forming something like a large emblematic jewel.

In other works trance takes over. In one sequence of her long series of photomat portraits overlaid with her calligraphy, Hiller took the original photographs of herself at midnight in the booths at railways stations and airports (eg., *Midnight, Baker Street*, 1983, *Gatwick Suite: Ascent/Flight/Descent*, 1983). Eyes often closed, head partially out of the frame or turned away from the viewer, hand sometimes barring the intrusive lens, the ecstatic configuration is clear, suggesting in these incongruous but ironically appropriate surroundings the inner transport of the mystic or the spirit flight of the shaman.

Of course the scriptorial *Sisters of Menon* is just as much a 'self-portrait' as the figurative images produced by the photomat. Each is framed by a different understanding of the 'automatic'. One of the deeply absorbing themes explored in this group of works is the conundrum of authorship. When the technique of automatic writing was adopted by the Surrealists in the first half of the last century, a distinction was made between its traditional use by mediums (whose writing purported to be dictated by another being) and the Surrealists' use (the writing originating from their selves and proposing the "unification of their personality").[16] "For us", André Breton wrote, "obviously the question of externality could not even be raised". In Hiller's *Sisters of Menon* both these approaches are combined, as aspects essentially of the same problem. The 'sisters of Menon' identify themselves as authors of the words, at the same time as Hiller, in her commentary, identifies them as part of a wider and truer understanding of her self. "My 'self' is a locus for thoughts, feelings, sensations, but not an impermeable, corporeal boundary. I AM NOT A CONTAINER". This would chime convincingly with Benjamin's evaluation of trance, and yet it would also suggest what a large component of subjectivity is involved in 'knowing' the universe. *Sisters of Menon* manifests, in utterly original format, an artist's 'vision' in the 1970s: a vision of solidarity and collectivity expressed in the metaphor of sisterhood, and linked to elemental nature and the antiquity of culture as something omnipresent and flowing: "*We are the Sisters of Menon / everyone is the sister / I am the sister / love oh the sisters … I live in the water / I live in the air – we are your sisters from Thebes*".[17]

In a work like *Elan* (1982), exactly the same spirit animates the abstract calligraphy, as well as the wordless singing that intersperses the sound tape which is heard as part of the same work. Here the artist's vision contrasts with that of the psychologist Konstantin Raudive, who in one sense shared the artist's interest in what is concealed or ignored on the margins of culture and perception but came up with very different results. In experiments during the 1960s Raudive left tape-recorders running in empty rooms and greatly amplified the 'silence', claiming to hear in the blur of mechanical and electronic noise the voices of the dead. We hear some of his recordings on the tape, their scratchy sound-fragments interrupting the sensuous continuity of Hiller's humming. The dead Raudive conjured up were selective: mainly famous male historical figures and a female 'helper'. His limitations were obvious, but Hiller was not concerned either to praise him as a scientific pioneer or to dismiss him as a crank so much as to treat his experiment as a metaphor – startling in its vividness – for the mixture of empiricism and imagination in all forms of knowing.

It is fascinating to reflect on the relationship between the 'imagined' others who contribute to the make-up of the self in *Sisters of Menon* and the 'actual' others whose images, dreams and testimonies are gathered in works from *Dream Mapping* and the early photomats, to *Witness* (2000), *From India to the Planet Mars*, and *Clinic* (2004). The earliest of these latter works involved a group of friends and one or two unknowns; the recent ones bring together a truly global hubbub. 'Imagined', 'actual': is the distinction so cast-iron? Does not a certain semantic ambiguity emerge from Susan Hiller's proposal of an enlarged notion of identity and knowledge? She has spoken of a "shared plight" confronting both artist and audience in the face of "our common cultural dilemmas".[18]

Hiller's practice erodes the supposed borderline between her 'solo' utterance and the collective of utterances revealed by her minute researches, whether manifested in sound, as multiple voices; in marks made by different hands; or formed from fragments of pottery or popular films. Her persistent attention to the tangled web of mediation in which we all pass our lives suggests that the artist's enquiries, experiments, projects and investigations in this sense figure as a model of how we all might begin to recognise and decipher the meshes of 'real' and 'constructed' which compose lived experience. In this way, "futures not otherwise possible can begin to shape themselves".[19]

Composite Group Dream Map

Night of August 23/24, 1974

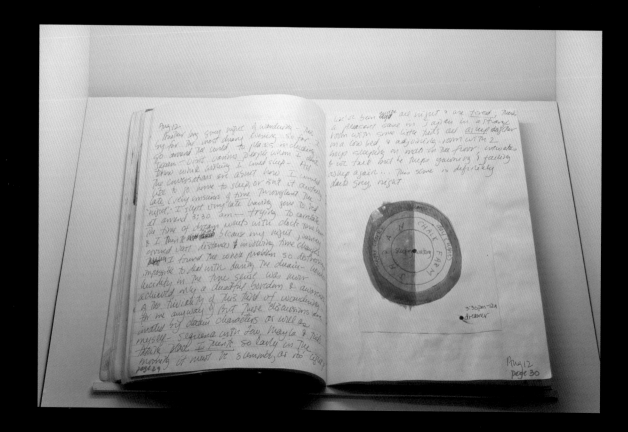

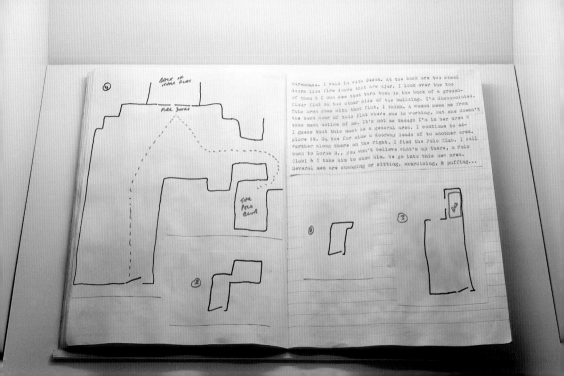

warehouse. I walk in with Susan. At the back are two steel
doors like fire doors that are ajar. I look over the top
of them & I can see that thru them is the back of a ground-
floor flat on the other side of the building. I'm disappointed.
This area goes with that flat, I think. A woman sees me from
the back door of this flat where she is working, but she doesn't
take much notice of me. It's not as though I'm in her area &
I guess that this must be a general area. I continue to explore it. On the far side a doorway leads of to another area.
Further along there on the right, I find the Polo Club. I call
back to Lorne B., you won't believe what's up there, a Polo
Club! & I take him to show him. We go into this new area.
Several men are changing or sitting, exercising, & puffing...

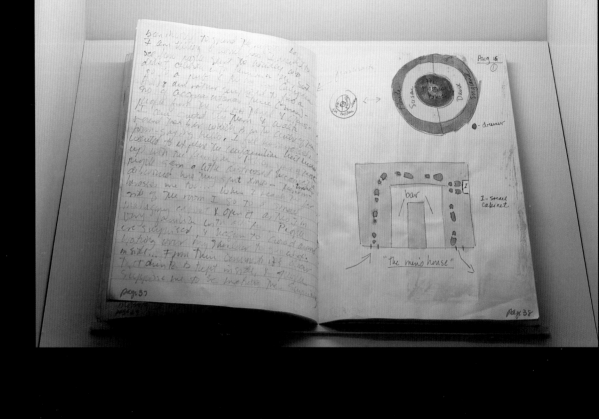

"the men's house"

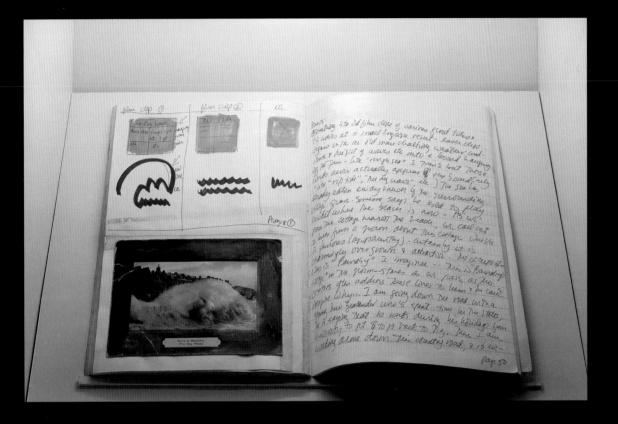

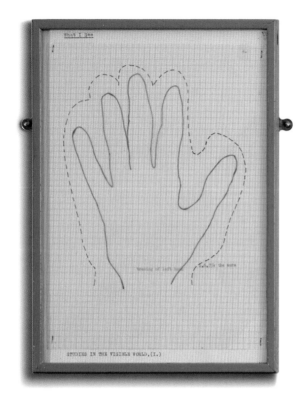

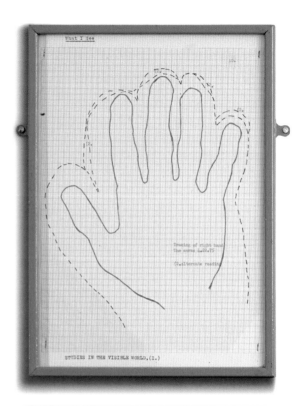

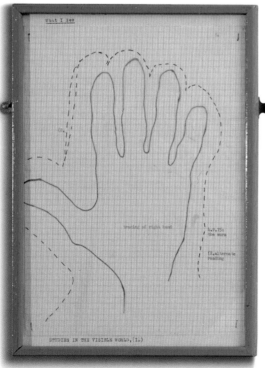

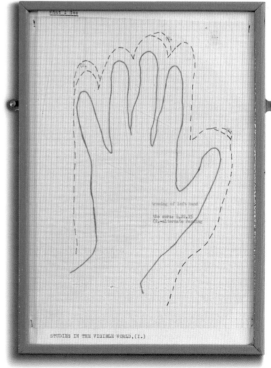

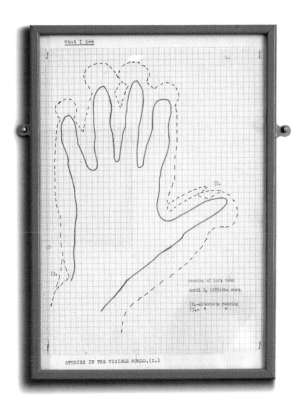

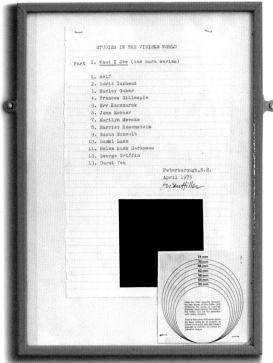

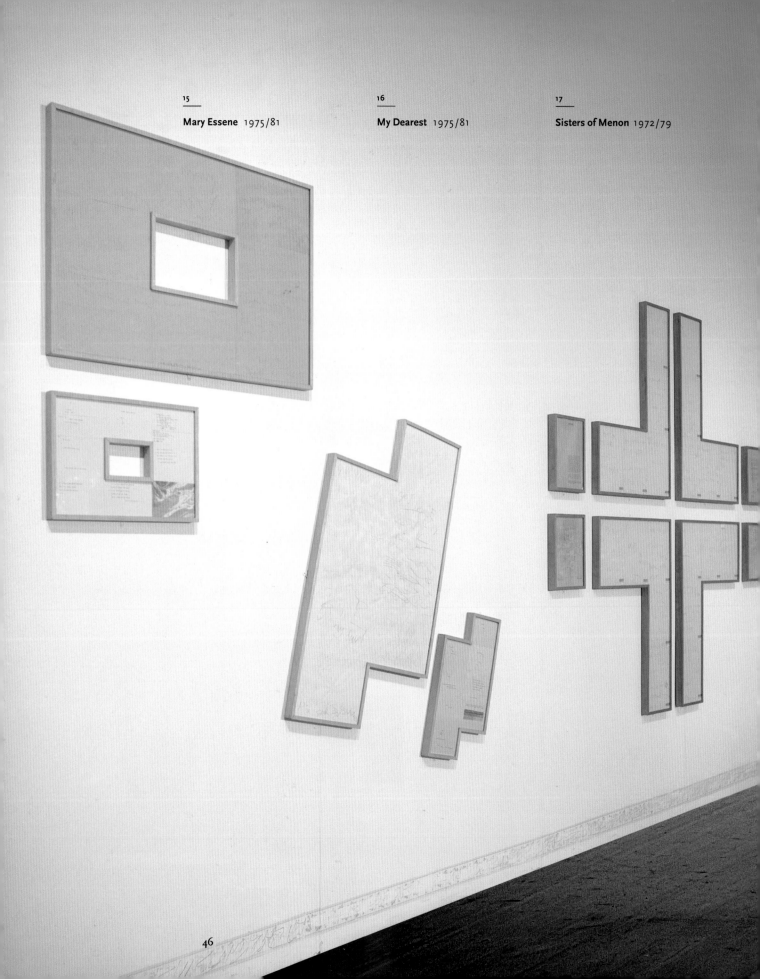

15 Mary Essene 1975/81

16 My Dearest 1975/81

17 Sisters of Menon 1972/79

46

18

So Don't Let it Frighten 1975/81

19

Get William 1975/81

20

Midnight, Baker Street 1983

installation at ICA, London 1986

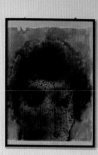

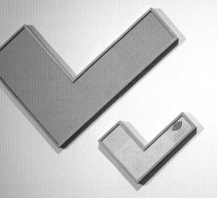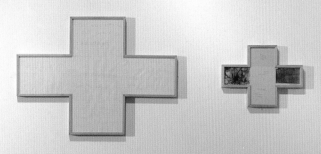

21

So Don't Let it Frighten 1975/81

GET WILLIAM

IS THE ONE FO

THE READER

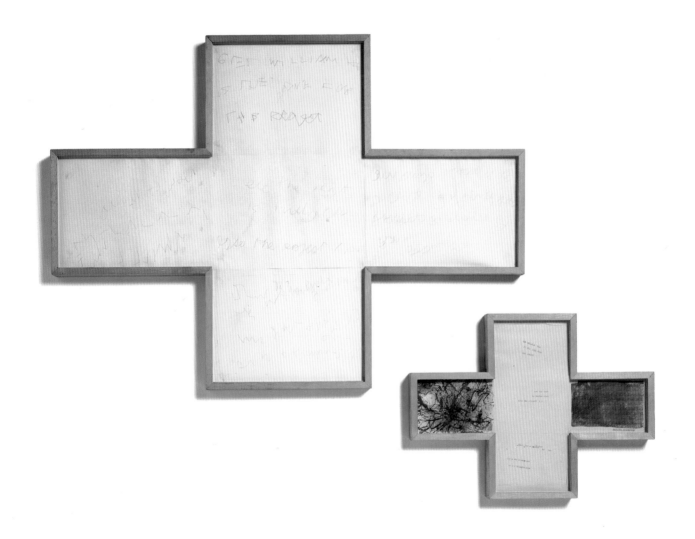

Self Portrait 1983

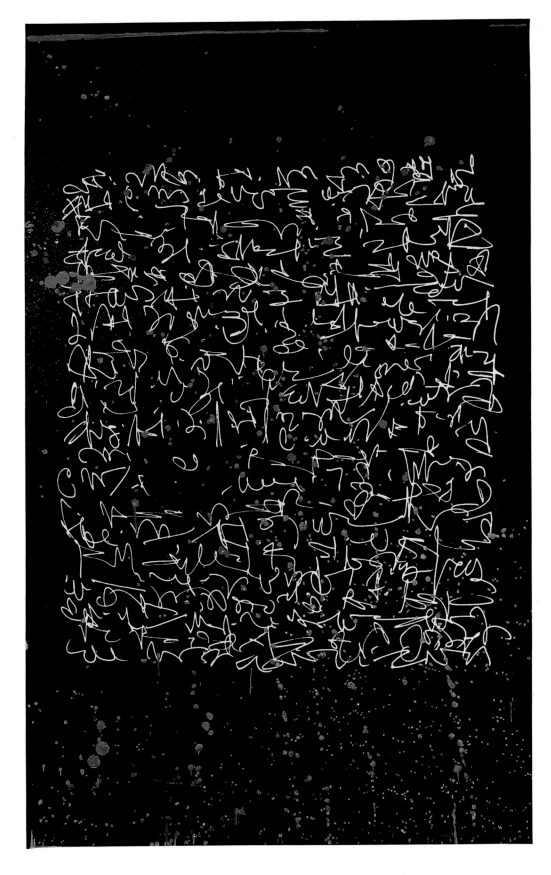

Autobiography 1983

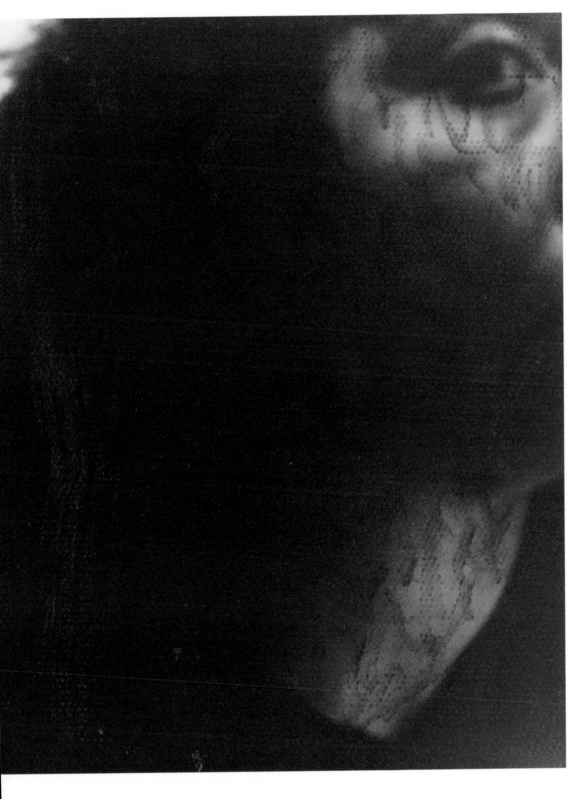

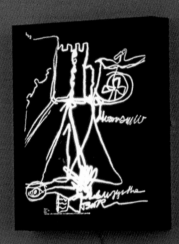

26

From India to the Planet Mars

1997–2004

27   [OVERLEAF]

From India to the Planet Mars

1997–2004, details

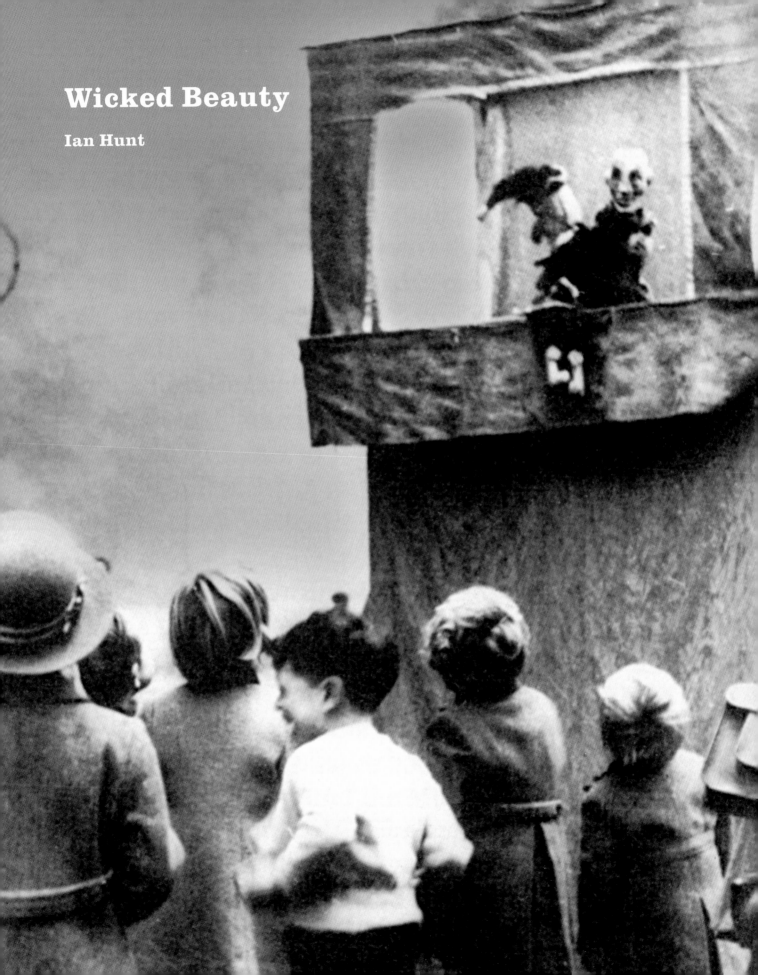

Wicked Beauty

Ian Hunt

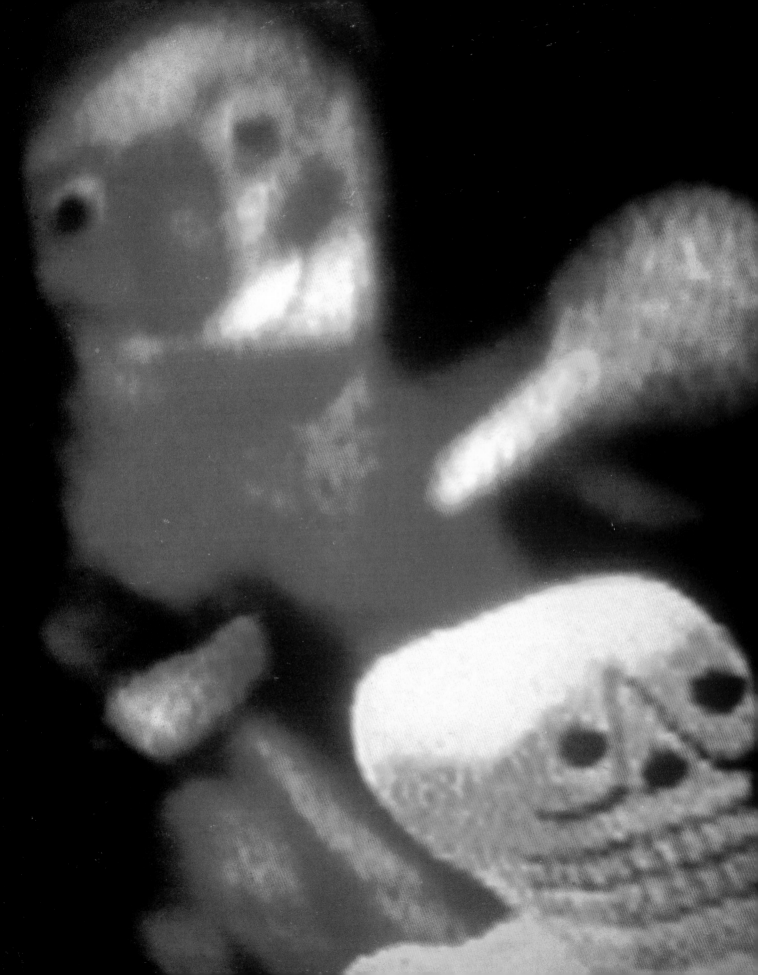

Wicked Beauty
An Entertainment

Ian Hunt

28 [OPPOSITE]

An Entertainment 1990

detail

They move too quickly for you to follow them and they surround you. They are bigger than you are. The dominant one has a screeching voice, distorted through something called a 'swazzle', but there is no mistaking that it belongs to a man. His eyes are painted and so the expression of his wooden face does not alter, whether he is tender or violent. His mood alternates without warning. *'Oh what a pity, what a pity.'* Though he can wheedle, coax and cajole, his painted eyes offer no insight into what animates him (their effect is quite unlike the coy, batted eyelids of the ventriloquist's dummy-child). He has small, carved hands, though they grip his stick effectively enough. Occasionally he lets us see his ridiculous swinging legs and tiny feet, but he remains bigger than we are. Of course, we know that he is animated by the hand of his master hidden in the booth, but that is too obvious an explanation. He is animated by something else – something *'wicked, wicked, wicked'*. He casts the word onto the heads of his opponents, relishing the accusation, but it returns on his own. His behaviour is child-like, in his lack of control of the desires that stir him; but he is frightening too, in that he gets away with it.

Punch, the red-faced, red-capped figure, not quite a jester in that he is also a family man, excites conflicting feelings. He is, by tradition, hunchbacked, his deformity an outward manifestation of his sins – his principal failing being anger. But he can be amorous and handsome. In the boxing match sequence of *An Entertainment*, the screen is split between magic lantern slides of Death in boxing gloves, facing left and right on different walls, and an upper compressed section in which Punch and Judy move towards each other from opposite sides in slow motion. The puppeteer calls out, 'On your left, Hungry Harry from Horsham. Take the bow. On your right, Dirty Dick from Deptford. First round. Shake hands.' Punch and Judy advance into a slow motion embrace or play-fight that you never quite get to see – a cut returns them to their corners to repeat the moves again. The passion and play aggression expresses itself in a slight quickening as they touch. The sequence, described in the post-production script as an 'entre-acte', also alerts the audience to the significance of the struggle between left and right. The 'little story of right hand, left hand, the story of good and evil' is excerpted from the soundtrack of *Night of the Hunter* (Charles Laughton's sole film as director), where it is narrated by a sinister preacher played by Robert Mitchum. To balance the impact of the preacher, a woman's voice (that of the apple-cheeked grandmother in the film) is then heard, praising the preacher's narration of the story and saying, 'I wish every soul in this community could get the benefit', which directs attention back to the other individuals with whom you are temporarily gathered to be entertained.

Susan Hiller's earliest plans for a work on Punch and Judy emphasised the question of its violence, the element that seemed most perplexing in a children's entertainment.

The piece is conceived to a scale that has an effect on adults as frightening as Punch and Judy can be for small children, and reawakens through this the ways in which early encounters with violence normalised in this way involve the learning of a disavowal. The puppets are taken out of the booth and its tiny proscenium and the viewer is immersed in unexpected sound, movement and action. Violence, however, was never the only issue. There is a concentration in *An Entertainment* on the domestic trinity of Punch, Judy and Baby. Older, mythic features of the story, such as Death, Devil and Hangman that imply the Christian framework of judgement, are preferred and later comic elements such as the policeman, sausages or dog Toby are excluded. Through the artist's meticulous process of editing, tender and ambiguous moments such as the repeated embrace emerge as particularly significant – so too, near the end of the piece, the way in which the illuminated baby floats up into the dark sky in slow motion and gently falls, all the time staying horizontal, its movement seemingly independent of the puppeteer's hands. Its sleep is not disturbed as it is tossed repeatedly into the air; the baby seems to be dreaming the unimaginable dreams that babies dream, as the darkness gives way to twinkling, coloured stars. As I respond to these images, I feel a combination of excitement, of co-responsibility for the drama that unfolds, and of passivity before it. One writer, trying to account for the paradoxical distribution of feelings predicated by the space of dreams, has formulated the question in this way: 'What manner of theatre is it, in which we are at once playwright, actor, stage manager, scene painter and audience?' Another, in an account of drama, noted that cry with which we reassure ourselves that what we behold in dreams is an illusion: 'It is a dream! I want it to carry on!'[1]

The perspective of the dreamer is significant in Hiller's work. In a talk from 1989, when filming of the Punch and Judy shows around seaside towns was underway, she said, 'I'm suggesting we acknowledge some perspectives of the dreamer, perspectives that are undermined as one speaks, in that, as a dreamer, you can be simultaneously the protagonist of the dream and the viewer watching the action on the screen of the dream. It's the sensation of being both inside and outside thought, of thought being both inside and outside one.'[2] Children, in watching a Punch and Judy show, learn to identify with the strong protagonist rather than with the objects and figures he attacks, as a way of 'enjoying' the experience that adults have offered them. But the experience of Hiller's piece itself does not, finally, rest with the ambiguous attractiveness and fearfulness of Punch. It is the experience of entering a darkened room and of not knowing what is going to happen next, or where. You are compelled to identify with the action as it unfolds, with whatever is happening around you, out of your control, rather than with specific characters. The four-wall set-up is too big. It is simply beyond your powers of projection or control as a viewer; you cannot identify with the mechanism of projection as you have learnt to do in a cinema in order to comprehend what you see. Here the movements enter you. This is just one of the ways in which the piece enables the viewer to see through a child's eyes: you are allowed little distance from the feelings and actions that enter you and animate you. As in a dream, the dreamer can be co-present in the stick, the baby, the wife, the man holding the stick, the echoing endlessness of the accordion music, or the stars in the night sky. A story by Ray Bradbury, *The Nursery*, 'in which the children's bedroom walls project whatever images they desire and finally become "real"'[3] has been mentioned by the artist as one of the incentives to make *An Entertainment* an encompassing environment in which images seem to move into the viewer's own space.

There are of course some sequences in which black and white footage isolates the puppets in the proscenium against a light backcloth, as though for study (this is in contrast to the way the granular coloured figures usually appear out of a darkened background, with no frame visible). The way footage of different performances revisits the stock characters and re-enters the narrative at different points also has the effect of opening out the Punch and Judy narrative, to some extent allowing the viewer to consider the phenomenon comparatively. But it is never possible to adopt a standpoint of distance. In one memorably disorienting sequence, labelled 'BAT sequence' in the post-production script,[4] the black and white footage is horizontally compressed and doubled so that the bottom inverted half of the projected image mirrors the top. The figures in chase from right to left to right and back again become part of a mobile abstraction, an expressionist cinema, Rorschach script. The doubled figure of Punch, whose red colouring registers as almost black on the black and white footage, becomes a graphic, flapping image, described by the post-production script as 'gestalt-like', which moves fast, right round and behind the viewer, forcing you to turn on the spot.

One other feature of *An Entertainment* should be mentioned, in that it seems to promise precisely that analytical distance from the phenomenon that the viewer can never quite attain. Before the show begins we are informed clearly and correctly by a woman's voice that: 'The texts spoken by the voices and the sound volume are exactly the same as in the original recordings. In order for the listener to become accustomed to the strangeness and rapidity of the speech, each utterance will be translated by an interpreter.' The voice is discernibly not that of someone for whom English was the first language. The voice of the other interpreter, a man, is differently accented and his emphases are sometimes unexpected. They are not archly scientistic (as in the slide-tape work *Magic Lantern* from 1987, where a woman's voice 'interprets' the words of famous dead persons from the recordings of a silent laboratory made by Konstantin Raudive), but they are not native English either. British viewers are perhaps being led to understand that this tradition can be seen as exotic, and that their reactions to it – even their ability to put words to the songs, their familiarity with Punch's catch-phrases and taunts and with the audience's responses – are part of what is being made available for study.

The voices of the two interpreters form yet another echoing of the dyad of female and male. The mythic dualities enacted by Punch and Judy shows came to fascinate the artist, in particular the way their meaning is dependent on the manipulation of two puppets at any one time by a single puppeteer. Punch, being present throughout, is a right-hand puppet, and all the other puppets with which he has stick-fights (Judy, Baby, Horse, Crocodile, Death, Ghost, Hangman or Devil) take their turn on the left hand. The boxing match (heard but not seen) is the only sequence where identical puppets are used on each hand. The duality of right and left (anciently aligned with good and evil, dextrous and sinister) is structurally present in Punch and Judy, but with no ultimate moral stability. And of course Punch, the triumphant right-hand puppet, appears to the audience on the left. This suggests to the artist that, 'everything in the unconscious (individual, cultural) may be ultimately reversible or that opposites change over when you're on the other side of the looking glass.'[5] One final note on the way mythic uncertainties are present even in fleeting improvisations of one of the puppeteers: at one point, Punch, confronted by Devil, says, 'You're Father Christmas', and promptly whacks him. When Hangman erects the gibbet Punch says, 'What's that, a Christmas tree?', as though he might be hoping for a present.[6] These jokes seem to come from an underlying uncertainty. They mirror our own difficulties in understanding whether these twenty-six minutes leave us with gifts of pity, fear or laughter.

In 1990/1991, when *An Entertainment* was first shown, it would be true to say that its technical means and immersive dangerousness were new. A press release issued by Matt's Gallery, commissioners of the piece, described it in an evocative tautology as a 'videobeam projection'. Quite apart from the newness of the projection technology itself, the work was edited across four programmes so as to move across four walls, and it utilised quadraphonic sound. The granularity of 8mm sound and image copied onto analogue videotape, and the edits, painstakingly cued by manual counting, were very real technical parameters within which the work was constructed. There are precedents in early cinema and animation (Vertov, Len Lye, Disney) for virtuoso rhythmic choreography, though here it is let loose around the four walls of a space by turns folded, compressed and opened out: a square space illuminated and reconfigured as a mental one. But the significance I registered here was not, at the time I first experienced *An Entertainment*, connected with that kind of reassuring formal and historical assessment. It was strongly emotional. I think I felt upset, though also strongly excited. I had emerged as white as a sheet, though plagued by no actual or falsely recovered memories, in as far as I understood what I had recognised in the work, or what, as it seemed, was in the work that had recognised me.

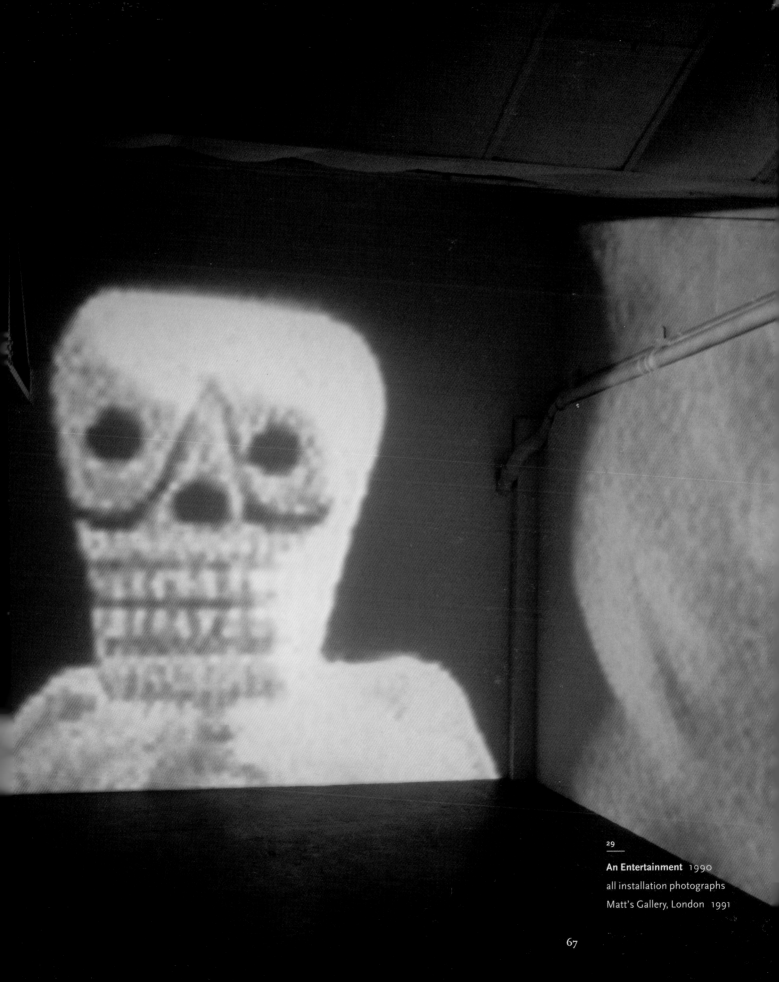

An Entertainment 1990
all installation photographs
Matt's Gallery, London 1991

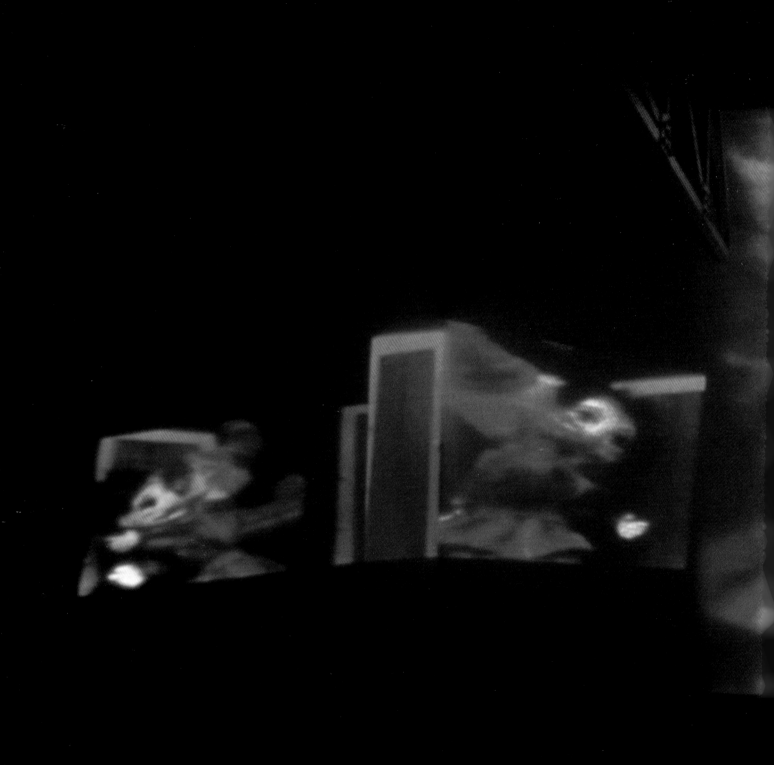

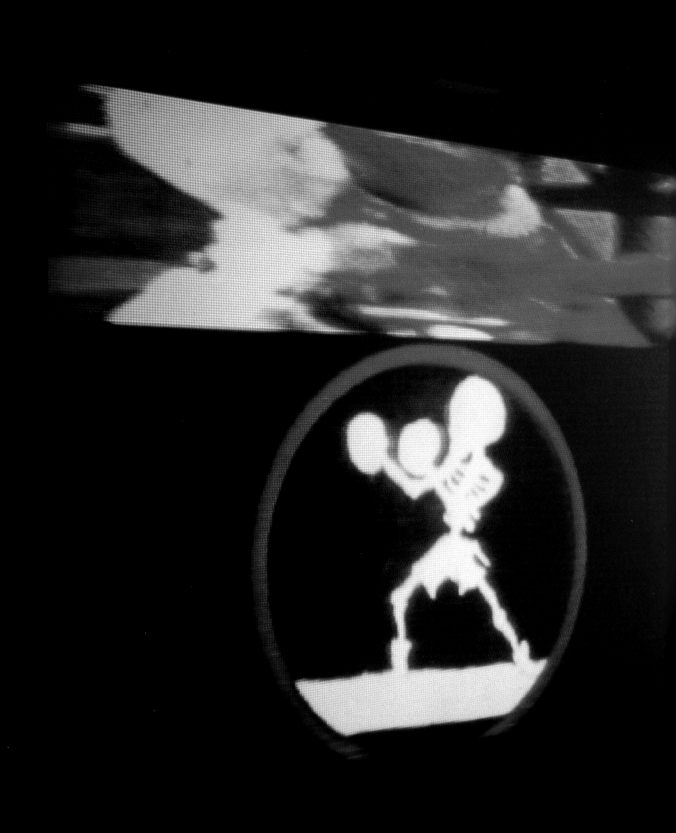

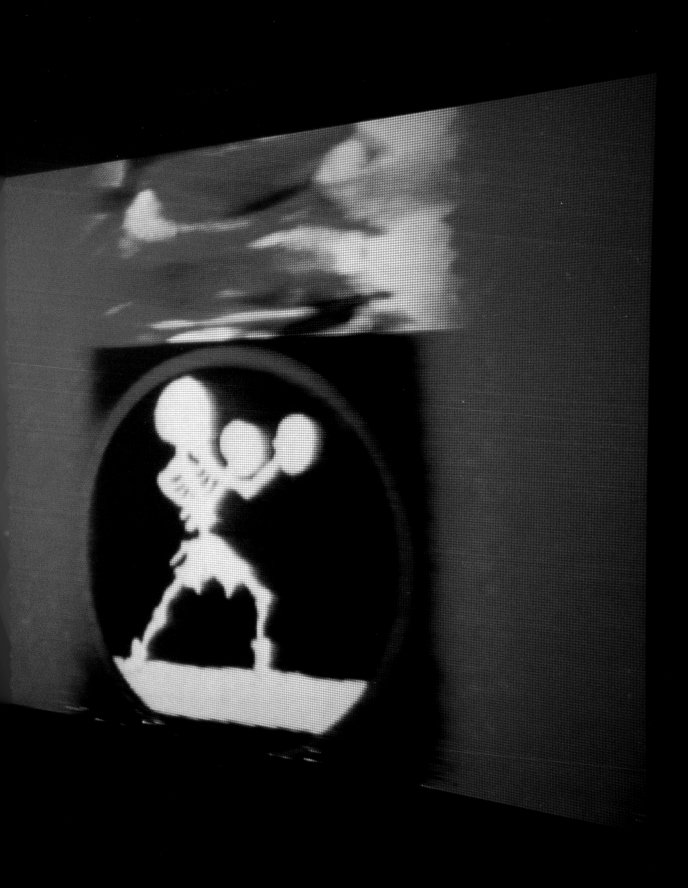

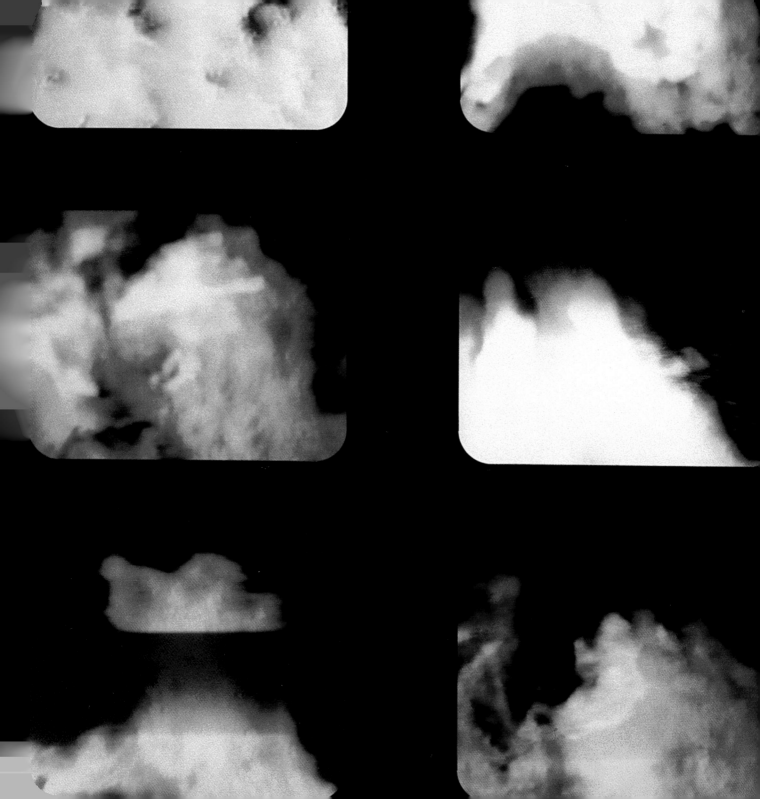

Before Testimony

Jean Fisher

*The use of the word 'subjectivity' is as enigmatic as the use of the word 'responsibility' –
and more debatable. For it is a designation chosen, in a way, to preserve our portion of spirituality.*
MAURICE BLANCHOT *The Writing of the Disaster*

In his later writings Adorno returned persistently to the theme that, after the catastrophe
signified by the name 'Auschwitz', we could no longer have faith in art as redemption from
a barbarism now revealed as inherent to Western 'civilisation'.[1] Not only was the assumption
of a 'disinterested' aesthetics based in instrumental reason ethically unsustainable, but so too
was representation itself: the trauma of catastrophe was unassimilable to artist and receiver
alike either as subjective experience or as representation except as a void of meaning.

Likewise, in the post-war decades, the response of artists was an increasing move
towards an emptying out of traditional aesthetic pleasure: on the one hand, the formal aus-
terity of 1960s Minimalism and Conceptualism that avoided social reference; and on the
other, Pop Art's surrender to the increasing influence of mass media in the construction of
collective consciousness and subjective identity. Concerned primarily with an interrogation
of the nature of art and its institutions, these practices did not however resolve the question
of art's responsibility, or better, answerability to life: in what way, if at all, can art bear witness to the unsayable, or void of meaning, in culture – to what, in its very repression, founds
culture's sense of itself? It was not until the generation of artists emerging from the socio-
political turbulence of the late 1960s and 1970s that the question begins to gain substance.
As Agamben notes, the aporia of Auschwitz is the very aporia of historical knowledge:
'a non-coincidence between facts and truth, between verification and comprehension',[2]
a lacuna at whose heart lies the mutual silence between the living being and the generic 'I',
or speaking subject of discourse, who is other to it; of the authenticity or 'truth' of testimony
and art. It is the resonance of this lacuna in Susan Hiller's work that is sketched out here.

At issue, as Walter Benjamin had already discerned, is the impoverishment of our
ability to have and communicate experience – that 'know-how' handed down by word of
mouth and condensed in the figure of the storyteller – or 'witness' – which was the foundation
upon which community traditionally built continuity, and whose transmissibility guaranteed
individual agency. Writing after the disaster of World War I he noted that, in a world of
communication devoted to the relay of mediated information, 'no event any longer comes to
us without already being shot through with explanation.'[3] Experiences like those of the
trenches or the Nazi death camps were so inconceivable to those who hadn't been there, so
impossible for the listener to incorporate into his or her everyday existence, that it put in crisis
the authority of the survivor's testimony. In his gloss on Benjamin, Agamben adds that 'today
the destruction of experience no longer necessitates a catastrophe, and that humdrum life in

30   [CHAPTER TITLE PAGE]

Belshazzar's Feast 1983/84
"Campfire Version", ICA, London
1986

31   [OPPOSITE]

Belshazzar's Feast 1983/84
details

any city will do... This does not mean that today there are no more experiences, but they are enacted outside the individual [who] merely observes them.'[4] He cites as illustration the tendency of tourists to give experience over to the camera, a dismissal of the body as the locus of authentic truth in favour of the machine inherited from Cartesianism. Like the witness to catastrophe, the evidence of experience gained through the senses, through the power of words and narration, is no longer trusted as possessing any *authority*: 'On the contrary, it is the character of the present time that all authority is founded on what cannot be experienced.'[5]

What we lose in this perpetual non-event of information is a sense of continuity and agency. As Agamben says elsewhere, in a traditional system, culture exists through its transmission: there is no discontinuity between past and present, old and new, because beliefs and values are bound into them. However, when traditional values lose their force, a gap emerges. 'Loss of tradition means that the past has lost its transmissibility, and so long as no new way has been found to enter into a relation with it, it can only be the object of accumulation' – the past becomes a monstrous and indecipherable archive.[6] Commodity culture attempts to fill this vacuum with a saturation of information, images, elaborated communications technologies, producing a confusion of spatial and temporal boundaries which collapses the distinctions between fantasy and reality, memory and experience.

Susan Hiller's work is both a critique of and a counter to the more dystopian implications of this scenario. Her work refuses the passivity imputed to the consumer of commodity culture and its surrender to the totalisation of meaning that instrumental reason imposes on everyday life – and by analogy any passive relation of artwork to viewer. On the contrary her work hollows out precisely that void of meaning that reason produces in its efforts to colonise and manipulate the subject's unconscious desire. It brings back into play a storytelling function articulated around testimonies of what, for reason, are the 'unsayable' experiences of the everyday that emanate from the interstices of popular culture.

Of the several versions of *Belshazzar's Feast / The Writing on Your Wall*, 1983–84, one presents a cluster of video monitors arranged to suggest a campfire around which, at night, one might gather to tell and listen to stories. The screen shows a constantly transforming curtain of flames that surges and fades in and out of the darkness to the aural accompaniment of crackling fire. As with the domestic hearth of the past, one becomes mesmerised by the flickering forms into a state of reverie, in which the imagination begins to invoke hallucinatory figures. A somewhat authoritarian voice ('What the fire says, Take One...') periodically introduces a faintly Arabic improvised vocalisation, alternating with a child's narration. Midway through the video, the soundtrack is punctuated by a whispered account of published newspaper reports by people who had claimed to receive transmissions from 'aliens' through the TV screen *after* the station had closed down broadcasting for the night. These 'messages' are often couched as terrifying premonitions of disaster, and it is almost as if the voice, while compelled to express the urgency of communication, was equally ashamed of speaking it aloud, as if it were some guilty secret.

The artist draws parallels between these hallucinatory TV transmissions and the phantasms of fire gazing, which were also often apocalyptic in tone, and links them with the Biblical story of Belshazzar's Feast, which tells how the King's punishment for transgressing divine law was forewarned in the form of a cryptic writing in light traced by a disembodied hand upon the wall: *mene mene tekel upharsin* – a 'meaningless' language that the mystic prophet Daniel was called upon to decipher. It is fragments of this story, articulated also through reference to the painting by Rembrandt, that reappear throughout the video, spoken in the often faltering voice of a young boy as if struggling to recall a lesson.

Hiller's juxtaposition of three modes of saying – a lilting glossolalia, or 'speaking in tongues', the authoritative voice of interpretation and the efforts of the child to relate the fragments of a story into a meaningful whole – realises the tension between the pulsions of desire and the constraints of instrumental language. The child's voice has particular significance here; his role also is as storyteller, or witness, and yet it is uncertain whether his struggle is to emerge from *infans* through narrativising culture, or, following Agamben's thought, whether the cultural itself is now in fragments and can only be imperfectly remembered and narrated. To be *infans* is to be without speech – a state common to both infants and the victims of torture for whom, as Elaine Scarry recounts,[7] the scenario of extreme bodily pain leads to a loss of language and therefore of subjectivity and community. It is a desubjectification whose most extreme condition Agamben attributes to those victims of the death camps who rarely survived, those known as the 'walking corpses', or 'Muslims' – those who, in relinquishing experience, had become no longer 'human'. Something analogous is alluded to in *Psi Girls*, 1999, a sound and video projection of manipulated fragments of popular films in which young girls experience paranormal and telekinetic phenomena. No longer children, but not yet adults, not yet fully 'human', they exist in a state of what in anthropology is called liminality, an in-between state of suspended space-time in which the chaotic libidinal drives have not yet been fully disciplined by the language of the social, such that the boundaries between self and world are experienced as indistinct and inarticulable except, as with the mystics, in a psychosomatic symptomisation.

In *Magic Lantern*, 1987, the triple slide projection assumes the role of the fire/TV of *Belshazzar's Feast* as a screen for inducing a hypnotic state. We are offered for contemplation the play of pure coloured light on a wall: rhythmic permutations of three discs of light, sometimes solo, sometimes overlapping, in three standard colours, red, yellow, blue, now small and discrete, now so large that they encompass the entire visual field. Two overlapping colours make a third; but three overlapping make a paradoxical multiplicity, One: white light. At moments all the colours seem to float in the air, in the mind's eye. Progressively we become aware that each individual colour is always contaminated by its 'other', the retinal afterimage; and as each colour fades, so its afterimage bleeds into the successive projection. The afterimage is a fleeting somatic effect of vision with no referent in the material world. It is therefore an experience conjured by us that cannot adequately be named despite its scientific 'explanation'; but we tend to become aware of it only in relaxed moments of reverie or other altered states when we lose sense of ourselves in an obscure liminal space-time 'outside' everyday consciousness.

The soundtrack, like that of *Belshazzar's Feast* draws on strange reports that have no 'rational' explanation, in this case the recordings of the Latvian psychologist Konstantin Raudive.[8] As with the flames of *Belshazzar's Feast*, we begin to imagine some coherent voice pattern in the chaotic hiss of tape noise as the introjected voices of 'interpreters', ethnographers or exorcists, attempt to impose a meaning on these inscrutable fragments. We catch glimpses of Hiller's subtle wit as the 'voice of Mayakovsky' appears in conjunction with a red disc of light, or that of 'Churchill' with blue (the dominant cultural colour symbols of the world's two contesting political ideologies – Left and Right). The Raudive recordings are interspersed with the artist's vocalisations, beginning with one voice, which quickly doubles into a four-fold polyphony producing an 'accidental' harmonics. The imprinting of sound in our minds fades with the soundtrack: a disintegration of time, like the 'voices of the dead', leaving only the barest echoes for Raudive/us to reinvent and reinvest with significance.

Magic Lantern takes up the paradox of the machine, especially recording and projecting devices, from the pinhole camera to various 'forerunners' of the slide projector itself. Whilst their scientific 'objectivity' was to provide the evidential truth of the world where the erratic experience of the human witness could not, at the same time devices like the magic lantern were used in Victorian popular entertainment for the projection of ghostly images from 'beyond the grave'. One might speculate that it was precisely to eliminate the disjunction between an indecipherable 'noise' of the world and the subject's desire to give it form and language that Raudive attempts to give over the role of witness to the machine as providing the incontrovertible evidence that subjective testimony lacks. But in the end the tapes can have no independent existence without his own witness to their veracity. And yet, as *Magic Lantern* reveals, the logic of instrumental language can never fill this lacuna because the human exists in a dual non-coincidental plane as embodied self and as subject in discourse.

Hiller returns to this paradox in *Dream Screens*, 1996, a work using the computer interface and designed to ensnare the wandering imagination of late-night Web surfers. This complex work draws on a number of discourses, including those of painting, the dreamwork and popular cinema, but, like *Magic Lantern*, it uses a seemingly simple visual format to provoke mental images. The user enters through a spiderweb-shaped colour palette where she can then choose to click into any one of a large range of colour fields, or let her imagination drift through the list of strange and often obscure pigment names to which each of these fields corresponds: 'Pure colour is the instrument of fantasy, the land of dreams for a child lost in games...' At the same time, she can choose from a selection of languages and listen to different, partially overdubbed layers of text: some are analytical, others are brief narrations, like recollected dreams, that derive from various films whose titles allude in some way to dream. The three 'passages' of the soundtrack are each accompanied by a signal corresponding to three modes of 'reality', from the distant to the intimate, that we witness indirectly through the intervention of machines: Morse code tapping out 'I am dreaming' (the unconscious), the radio picture of a pulsar, the remnant of a Supernova explosion (the cosmos), and a heartbeat (the somatic). The model is the labyrinthine game of infinite couplings and flows, the shift between structure (the finite) and the event (the indefinite), which, despite its logical origins, is the nature of cyberspace itself as well as of the inscrutable workings of memory, dream and art. If vision is finite, the play of the visionary is unbounded by either time or space.

These works reveal the indeterminacy between our experience of reality and non-reality. Nothing is real here in a material sense except the experience of the work itself. Conscious and unconscious processes fold into one another; the linear co-ordinates of cause and effect collapse into a constant becoming-present of the past and becoming-past of the present. It is a mapping of the self's becoming-other than itself that is topological not historical: the subject is what the intuition produces.

Oscillating throughout is the disjunction between voice as hieroglyph and the voice of reason that constantly intercedes but ultimately fails in its explanations. Belshazzar's scintillating inscription *mene mene tekel upharsin*, Hiller's vocalisations, the 'voices' in Raudive's tape hiss and the murmuring glossolalia that we experience as we approach the myriad suspended miniature speakers of *Witness*, 2000, qualitatively relate to mystic speech and the 'speaking in tongues' of Pentecostal church singers. Like the fire itself, they are inarticulable testimonies to an enchantment; they signal the indecipherable language of the 'spirit', an experience of 'possession' that can 'make sense' only by re-narrating it as if it appeared, like 'alien transmissions', to emanate from outside the subject. 'Language, in order to bear witness', as Agamben says, 'must give way to a non-language in order to show the impossibility of bearing witness.'[9]

Clearly what is important in Hiller's voices and hallucinatory images is not the 'message' (which is indecipherable or a product of our imaginings) but that something takes place, an act of enunciation, which paradoxically can only take place through the destitution of the subject. The extreme limit of this destitution is the figure of the 'muslim'; but desubjectification is the implicit condition upon which the speaking subject founds a place from which to speak. Catherine Clément called this suspension of the subject and signification 'syncope', a momentary loss of breath, an eclipse of consciousness, a rhythmic dissonance, but also the moment of artistic insight from which a new work is born,[10] – testimony made possible through an 'impossibility of bearing witness'. It is through the revelation of this lacuna in testimony and storytelling that Hiller's work restores the transmissibility of culture and may be said to be answerable to life. In its suspension of the rational subject it enables us to grasp the traumatic void of meaning that haunts our memories of the everyday, a truth of the world that opens up a space of transformation and action.

32

Belshazzar's Feast 1983/84

s.m.a.k., Ghent 2004

Belshazzar's Feast 1983/84

Fundación Eugenio Mendoza,

Belshazzar's Feast 1983/84
California State University
Museum, Long Beach 1988

Magic Lantern

Magic Lantern 1987
Tate Gallery Liverpool 1996

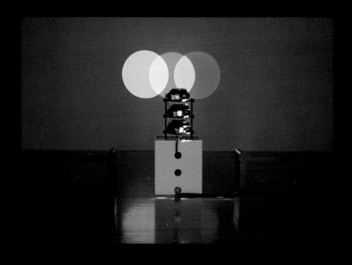

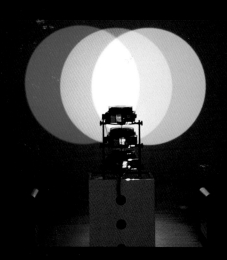

Magic Lantern 1987

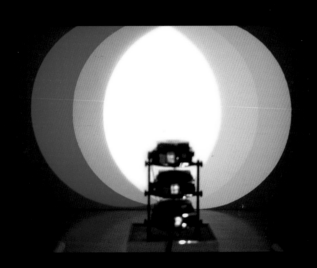

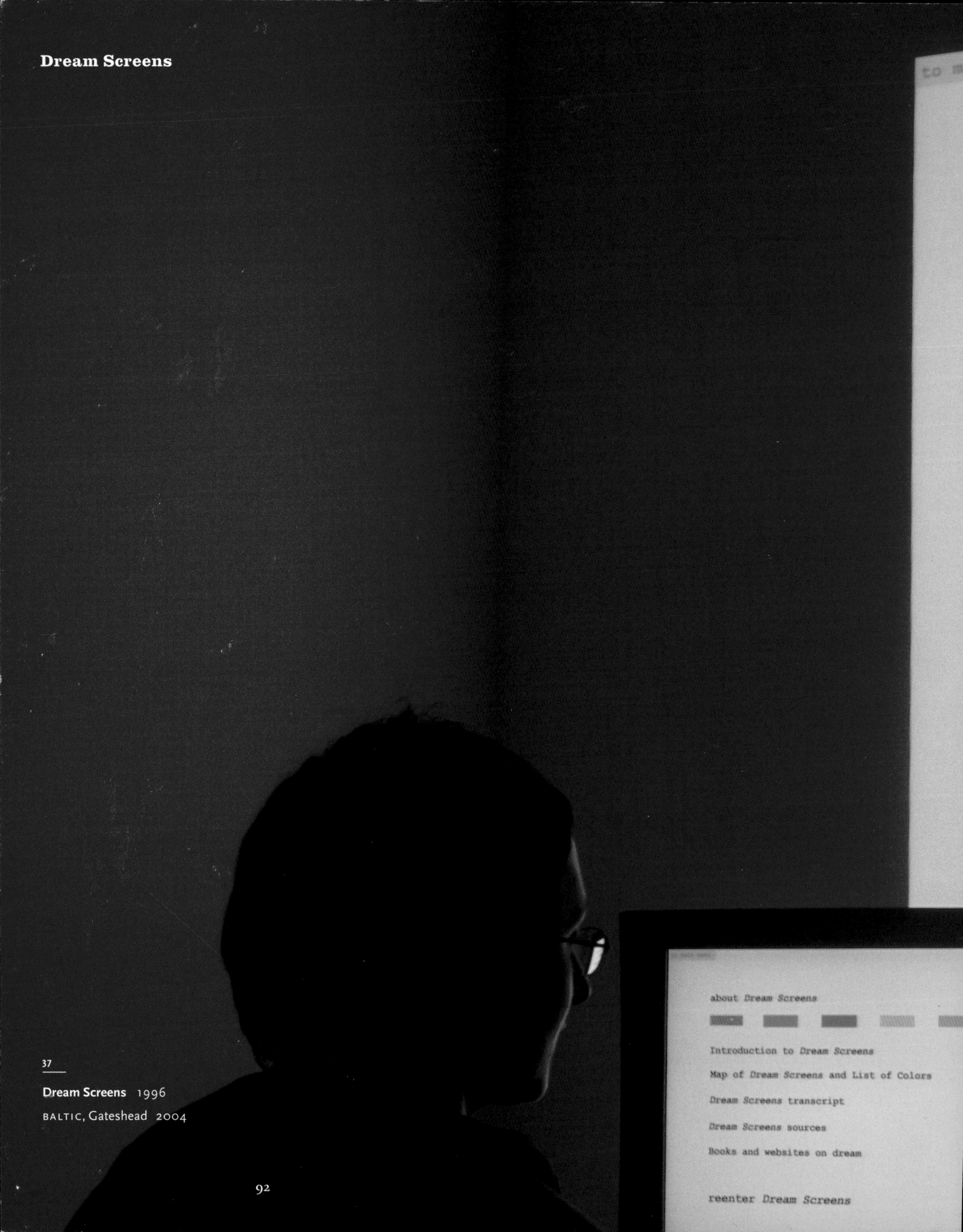

to

about *Dream Screens*

Introduction to *Dream Screens*

Map of *Dream Screens* and List of Colors

Dream Screens transcript

Dream Screens sources

Books and websites on dream

reenter *Dream Screens*

37
___

Dream Screens 1996
BALTIC, Gateshead 2004

about *Dream Screens*

Introduction to *Dream Screens*

Map of *Dream Screens* and List of Colors

Dream Screens transcript

Dream Screens sources

books and websites on dream

enter *Dream Screens*

a *Dream Screens* book, please print the five documents located in the folder "artistbook

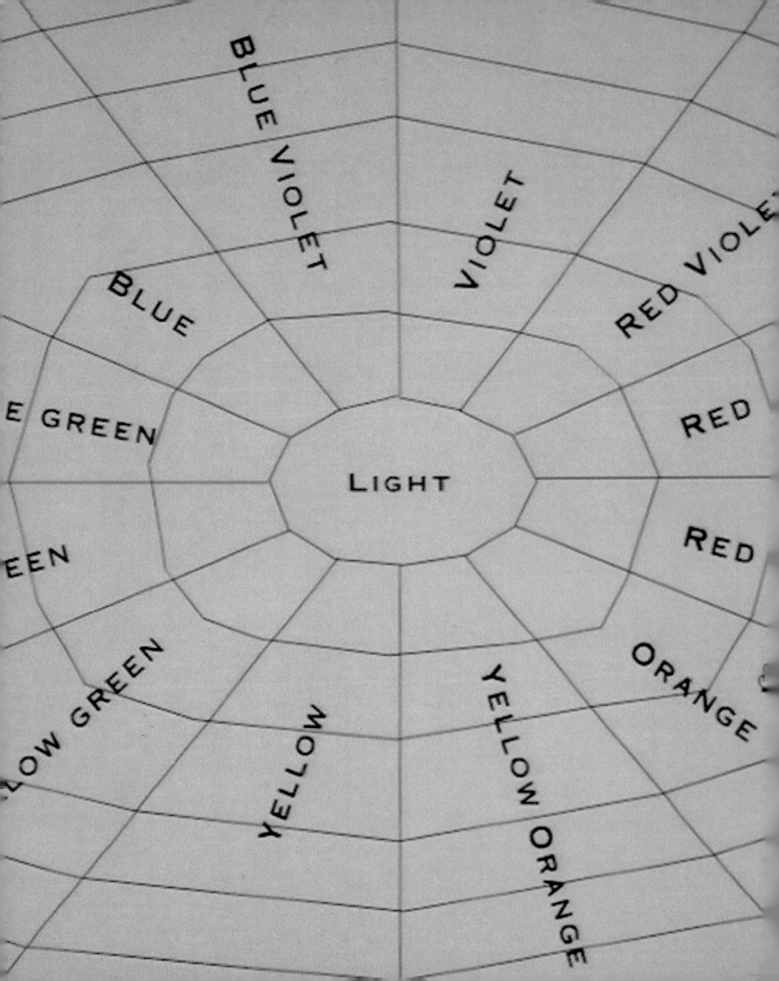

"...scarce stains the dust..."

Denise Robinson

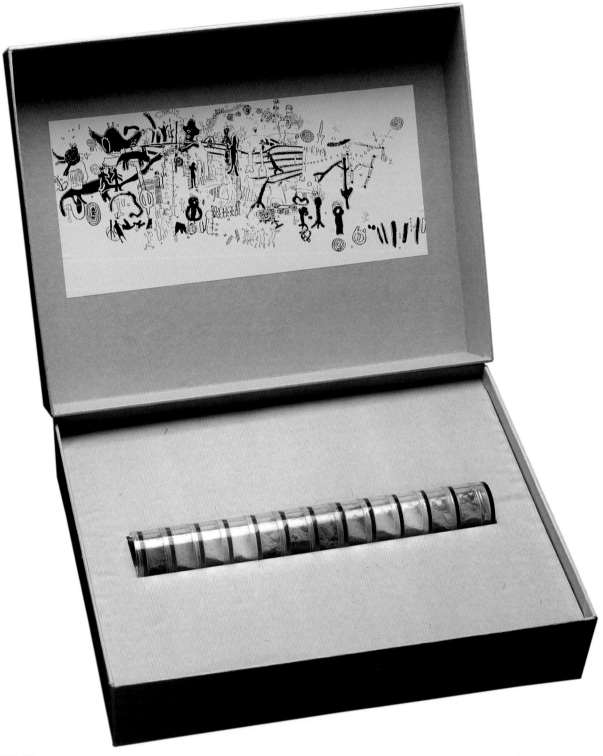

From the Freud Museum 1991–97
Nama-ma / mother

"…scarce stains the dust…" [1]
Freud's Museum – the Work of Susan Hiller

Denise Robinson

*The shock is the jolt of power acquired by things when they lose their transmissibility
and their comprehensibility within a given cultural order.* [2] GIORGIO AGAMBEN

*The category of the 'other' includes the inhabitants of the realms of supernatural beings and monsters,
the territories of real or imaginary allies and enemies, and the lands of the dead – places far from the
centre of the world, where one's own land is, and one's own reality. The 'other' is always distant as well
as different, and against this difference the characteristics of self and society are formed and clarified.* [3]
SUSAN HILLER

Susan Hiller locates her work within the terrain on which so much has been built – and lost –
in a debate on difference, which seems always haunted by a need for that final resolution of
difference. The citation from Agamben, itself passing through citations of Walter Benjamin –
opens up pathways to the fragments that constitute Hiller's entire body of work but which take
on particular significance in encountering the various incarnations of her projects related to the
Freud Museum: *At the Freud Museum*, exhibited at the Freud Museum in Maresfield Gardens,
London in 1994, the subsequent book, *After the Freud Museum* published in 1995 [4] and the
gradual scaling up the work in the following versions exhibited as *From the Freud Museum*.

Hiller offers her own version of the museum in her afterword to *After the Freud Museum*:
"What I think is positioned here is an extended and episodic view of my personal sense of
inhabiting an historically-specific museum of culture with permeable boundaries, which
might as well be called 'the Freud Museum'", [5] and she does so by appropriating the appro-
priative conceits of all Museums – here through a mimicry of the archiving techniques of
the archaeological museum in a way that permeates every aspect of the work's realisation:
*002 Ευχη/prayer, presented, 1991, photocopied map; tesserae and modern marble slab found at the
entrance to the underworld near Vathia, in customized cardboard box, labelled [25.5 x 33 x 6.5 cm].*

Archaeological collecting boxes are used and intricately constructed to hold, protect and
display vulnerable, unique objects, as though from an archaeological dig, the interior of each
box is tailored for the specific requirements of each artefact which, in this instance includes:
*an emblem in the form of a sweet for the Royal Wedding of Diana and Charles; a ouija board; 4 bars
of soap marked 'MADE IN ENGLAND'; a pamphlet on the suffering of the Jewish minority in
Roumania; earth samples from the 6 counties of Northern Ireland* … all torn from their context to
be immaculately installed and sealed within each box and then within vitrines. Paradoxically
it is this process of framing that completes the tearing of the objects from their contexts –
becoming quotations in which Agamben recognises, "The particular power of the quotation
arises, according to Benjamin, not from their ability to transmit the past and allow the reader
to relive it, but on the contrary from their capacity to make a clean sweep, to expel from the

38   [CHAPTER TITLE PAGE]

From the Freud Museum 1991–97
Experimental Art Foundation,
Adelaide 1998

context, to destroy".[6] Hiller's work opposes the inheritance of the 19th Century roots in the museum which forces its objects into a taxonomy of compliance, yet there is no post-colonial duty being enacted simply to suture something back into place; the very nature of the fragment refuses this. After gathering these materials and objects through a specifically charged archival system, which in its initiation fantasised the power of recording, Hiller creates a hyper-consciousness of their new status – a living breach.

As people gather to view *From the Freud Museum*, within say, its presentation at Tate Modern – a museum within a museum – they are silhouetted against the illumination of the vitrines, moving slowly, looking closely, absorbed in a kind of self-circuiting, ruminating meditation. What the beholder encounters when looking into the vitrines – however uniformly ordered, however much the promise of knowledge of rare and precious objects is suggested – is a shift in the cultural order: "the esoteric and the everyday, the mystical and the profane, theological categories and materialistic categories".[7] The fragments spread throughout the boxes, their context destroyed and by now lost to their transmissibility in their 'given cultural order', nevertheless re-presented again, 'once more'. Although there are often parallel documents, they are oblique to the meanings of the object they attend. There are no explanatory texts, and although the framing is carefully elaborate there's no continuity, no way of tying the fragments into an existing circuit or historical trajectory, leaving the beholder to be drawn into an encounter, to ask, "what is it doing here, with me?" – an unknowing encounter with their own 'secret self'. In a world lost to ritual, it's a gentle trick, a sleight of hand by the artist, playing out the infinite impressions – those points of contact – that make up Hiller's, and perhaps all our archives.

Hiller's resistance to incorporation within the dynamic of cultural history is beautifully articulated in the first of the boxes, *Nama-ma (mother)*. This is a reference to cave paintings at Uluru by Australian aborigines and also the first box recorded in her book *After the Freud Museum*.[8] This elaborately detailed book where records, categories, histories, memories and modes of forgetting all coalesce, begins with the image of a container which holds Australian native earths, found at Papunya – with the help of Papunya artists. It is accompanied by a text, which says, "The title means 'Mother' in an Aboriginal language I can't speak or understand". To have here, as both the object and the subject of her work, representation of distance and its untranslatability, is an indication of the very moving ambivalence which lies at the heart of her work.

I saw the book *After the Freud Museum* before I first encountered its display at Tate Liverpool in 1996, knowing that it was a reviewing / re-working of the material of her installation of 22 boxes *At the Freud Museum*. Yet this work (extended by this time to 44 boxes, re-titled *From the Freud Museum* and installed at the entrance to the retrospective) introduced the rest of the exhibition by refusing a sense of going-back-in-time: because this 'last' work allows for what Benjamin called "reading history backwards". In this process another feature of history is disturbed, for these projects are not only related to the historical effects of psychoanalysis and the twentieth century's internalising of Freud's thought, because with the lightest touch they undermine the stability of the object, the fulcrum of cultural history. Hiller's project it seems is not to elevate a historical moment – as has occurred through the historicising of Surrealism's relation to Freud's work on dreams – nor to overcome or intervene in it, but to conjure a kind of sympathetic magic formed by an ambivalent relation to the kinds of knowledge that this history has produced.

Lacan's work too inhabits Freud's museum, albeit in a different incarnation and via another trajectory: as a necessary intervention into the materialist, idealising appropriation of Freud's work. Lacan re-articulated Freud, connecting the social and the psychic, showing that we cannot, as the terrible aphorism says 'live the dream'; "the real has to be sought beyond the dream – in what the dream has enveloped, hidden from us, behind the lack of representation".[9] The real *is* the missed encounter.

The collection of cultural artefacts in *From the Freud Museum* includes debris derived from Freud's archives, his magic lantern slides and other slides, which Freud left uncategorised. In replicating them as 35mm slides and cataloguing them into types, Hiller suggests that the function of Freud as collector becomes transformed because her boxes now hold objects from Freud's home, of entirely different orders: *Scientific specimens; Miniature curiosities; Traditional magic lantern slides; Early Disney cartoon strips.*

They have become part of her own collection – but then they always were. It strikes me that Hiller's mimicry of the history museum via Freud is also like Benjamin's understanding of mimicry – that the very power of the copy is its influence over what it is a copy of. Their method of containment and the chronology of their making is not parodic but has the effect of gently mocking the processes and hierarchy of 'cultural history'. It is this gentleness which is significant as this mimicry does not challenge, but collapses its logic by extending the classificatory processes of the museum: *Presented, 1991; Filed, 1991; Realised, 1991; Displayed, 1991; Boxed, 1993; Positioned, 1994; Located, 1994; Remaindered, 1994; Represented, 1994.*

The distinction between debris and archive is not simply blurred here, for there is something at stake in this distinction which echoes that found in Freud's collection displayed in the 'domestic' museum of his home, including carefully categorised precious stones, figurines and ethnographic artefacts chosen for the continuity of their subject matter, regularly revised and replaced. Hiller has shown us that they also include a more random, less cohesive range of objects. Once the logic of Freud's collection is disturbed in this way then it shows, as she says, that the category itself becomes the artefact and all sources can become archives: *The street; Tabloids; Museums; Toy shops; Magazines; Cinema; Texts; Rubbish skips.*

The collector is not a benign figure. On the contrary the figure of the collector transgresses for "he questions the hermetic self-sufficiency of various disciplines...breaking with an historical view of the past...where truth lay in extremes through his unique archive on the history of caricature, erotic art, and the portrayal of manners". For Benjamin – referring to the collector Edward Fuchs, "It was the collector who found his way into (these) grey areas... where the models of art history sooner or later came to grief."[10] This scenario of the collector does not mistake cultural history for history; rather it opposes any model of cultural history, and by focusing on the marginal object it disturbs the logic of continuity.

In my discussions with Susan Hiller I attempted to define the nature of the objects she works with, and suggested that she was in a sense re-ordering Freud's collection. "I thought my collection...was in the gaps of the things left out. There's Freud and then there's the Freud Museum and then there's contemporary uses and versions of Freud and all of these things were in play – but starting with the notion of collecting, which is something everybody does when they are a child... I came up with a very different solution because everything that I started with was already a fake or a replica or something of no value or of a different order of value."" Hiller's Freud project, then, became not so much a consideration of the nature of the objects. The 'strange power' of the object came from a form of collecting while registering that something was missing.

Collecting is of course not a signature of Hiller's alone, but an element which is unremitting throughout 20th century art. Nor is my writing here an attempt to describe her work as a form of mastery or exemplary of the collector, it is more relevant to say that the collector shadows the figure of the artist. Hiller in a sense knows that she does not know what she wants but finds it nevertheless and it is this action which allows for the recognition of the inarticulate and repressed within the paradigm of cultural history.

The Fluxus artist George Maciunas, a refugee from Eastern Europe, up until his death accumulated elaborate forms of information to create a graph, the design of which could ultimately map all 'world art'. In attempting to map the thing that cannot be contained, he mapped the very anxiety of death and burial. Maciunas' mapping of culture was compelled by his fear of its burial; this burial is precisely where Hiller's work registers. It comes close to a form of archaeology described by Kenneth Reinhard in his discussion of Freud. In the process of attempting to describe the theory of psychoanalysis to his patient 'Rat Man', pathologised as obsessive, "Freud's own re-writing of the meaning of archaeology was made in reference to his own collection...they were, in fact only objects found in a tomb, and in their burial had been their preservation; the destruction of Pompeii (through the eruption of Vesuvius) was only beginning now that it had been dug up."[12]

Measure by Measure (1973 – ongoing) also prefigures the work of *From the Freud Museum*, holding within a museum case the remnants of the primary art form of the Western canon, painting – but paintings that did not survive the machinations of the historicising process. For, just as the Diana and Charles emblem or the desert soils of Uluru pass through the irreversibility of "quotation" so do these paintings. In Hiller's terms they have been 'analysed': burnt, reduced to ashes. The ashes are now contained within some 30 burettes, casting their shadow through the museum case onto the gallery wall, echoing the inference in all her work: these ashes become the substance for the shadow of the paintings and as in all Hiller's work plays out the relation between destruction and preservation.

A screened film, one of the most ephemeral and most difficult mediums to incorporate in this or any archive, is in a sense 'captured' in *From the Freud Museum* – through both its projection and its miniaturisation. A loop of Hiller's film *Bright Shadow* is dimly screened onto the gallery wall at the edge of the vitrines and simultaneously played on a miniature television monitor installed in one of the boxes. What we see in this film and all analogue film, is the effect of what we do not see: a series of film frames that are occluded through the speed of their movement; now a montage of fragments, it is returned here as one more fragment in the process of being archived: *022 Séance / seminar, edited, 1994, photocopied engraving from Athanasius Kircher,* Ars Magna Lucis et Umbrae, *1671; miniature television monitor (l.c.d. type), showing a programme by the artist entitled* Bright Shadow, *in customised cardboard box, labelled (25.5 x 33 x 6.5 cm).*

There is an encounter here with the fantasy of containment and it is not just with regard to the objects but the collective potential of the work, a desire to both 'catch' and release something through the interstices. Hiller reiterates this: "... I have said the Freud Museum work is a film – 50 frames, and in the spaces between the frames, people construct their stories... I always wanted to 'catch' people in the gaps, the gaps between discourses and the gaps between frames, in this work quite literally".[3] The idea that in the dimly illuminated film of shadows hovering at the edge of the vitrine something has escaped, brings us back to the artist's encounter with the museum, appearing as a gesture that challenges the contemporary Museum's forms of containment, including the increasing amount of interpretive material which the beholder now encounters.

These gaps or ellipses are in all of Hiller's work but have a particularly vivid realisation in her automatic writing experiments. They also call up the history of Surrealism's preoccupation with automatic writing. The historicisation of Surrealism – which never promised a peaceful night – is formed largely by ignoring the splits within it and are significant here for a consideration of Hiller's positioning her work in opposition to automatic writing as a form of possession often feminised and pathologised as hysteria. Hiller shows not what the symptoms of hysteria expresses but how it serves the expressive powers of others for her automatic writing experiments take the idea of expression itself to task.[4] The French Surrealists' preoccupation with the unnameable in the muse is precisely what Hiller deflects, for she returns her experiments back through that which names them. These experiments include: *The hand tinted writing of an autistic child – autistic automatism; A colour Xerox of a Jackson Pollock – artistic automatism.*

"... I've worked by collecting objects, orchestrating relationships, and inventing fluid taxonomies, while not excluding myself from them". Just where that 'self' is can be approached through the work of Gertrude Stein. Experimenting with automatic writing while at Harvard in 1896 she describes that she became "the perfect blank while someone practice(d) on her as an automaton." As Alan Weiss remarks, that 'someone' was herself. After, when Stein noted the high degree of repetition in her automatic writing experiments where, "the voice seemed that of another person", Weiss notes, "She was certainly not repeating 'herself'".[5]

Between the first entry and the last – in *From the Freud Museum* and its recording in the book *After the Freud Museum* – is an archive so diffuse that the places from which the fragments of texts, objects and forms come, the kinds of materials and modes of recordings, and the time of their 'burial' and recovery, approach a new threshold. The last entry in the book, RELEQUIA (relic) is a recording of the box which holds a quotation by Walter Benjamin and an artificial corsage, "made in USSR occupied Germany". For Benjamin, the collector had a relation to history which defied its forward trajectory as defined by the object of cultural history, and here he relates it to what is at stake in remembering. The words of Walter Benjamin: "To articulate the past historically does not mean to recognise it 'the way it was'. It means to seize hold of a memory as it flashes by at a moment of danger." This text placed beside the corsage also disperses the identity of the 'enemy' and alters the orientations of history.

Or look to box No 48, the tiny transparent coffin become a vitrine, holding within it a dead praying mantis, someone's pet. Parallel to the coffin sits the record of a discussion in the 1970s to establish an 'inter-governmental body' to enquire into the increasing number of reports by people who have seen extra terrestrials. It brings a smile, the 70s! – but Hiller's associative circuit extends to where 'mantis' is related to mantic, which is divination or prophet while connecting this U F O phenomena to a Salvationist myth.[16] This momentary contact between a symbol of mortality – through a mimicry of death – with the desire for redemption is possible because they have been torn from their place, their context destroyed.

The power of the fragment destroys the past in order to re-live it, and it is this that echoes throughout the many permutations of *From the Freud Museum* extending throughout all of Hiller's work; through dream states, the techniques of automatic writing, the shifting transmissive powers in new technologies which precipitate radical shifts in consciousness, or the channels of mass media where she tears fragments from the pop body of modernity. Then there is the overlaying of the configurations of the sacred and profane, all present again in her video and auditory installations, including, *An Entertainment, Wild Talents,*[17] *Witness* and *Psi Girls,* all of which embalms, in an inexhaustible archive, the shock of the moment of their un-transmissibility. Hiller returns the impressions which result back, within the permeable walls of her museum, wherever it may be.

First change of all a fragment comes away from another ruin and with slow fall scarce stains the dust
SAMUEL BECKETT [18]

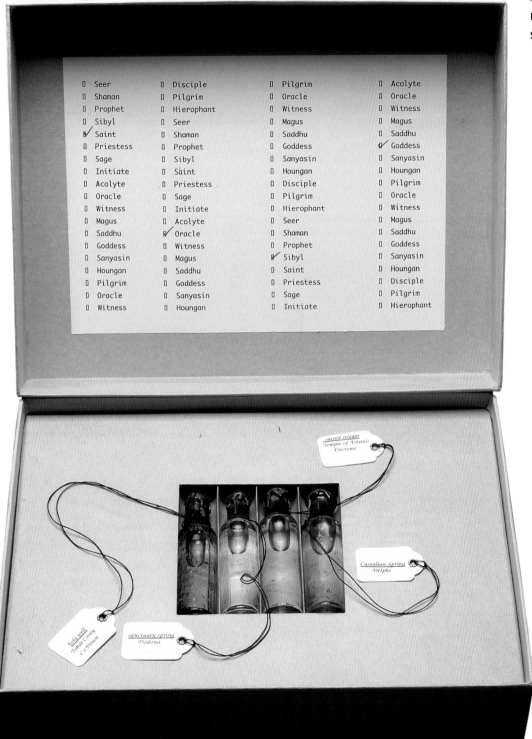

From the Freud Museum 1991–97

Hayward Gallery, London 1997

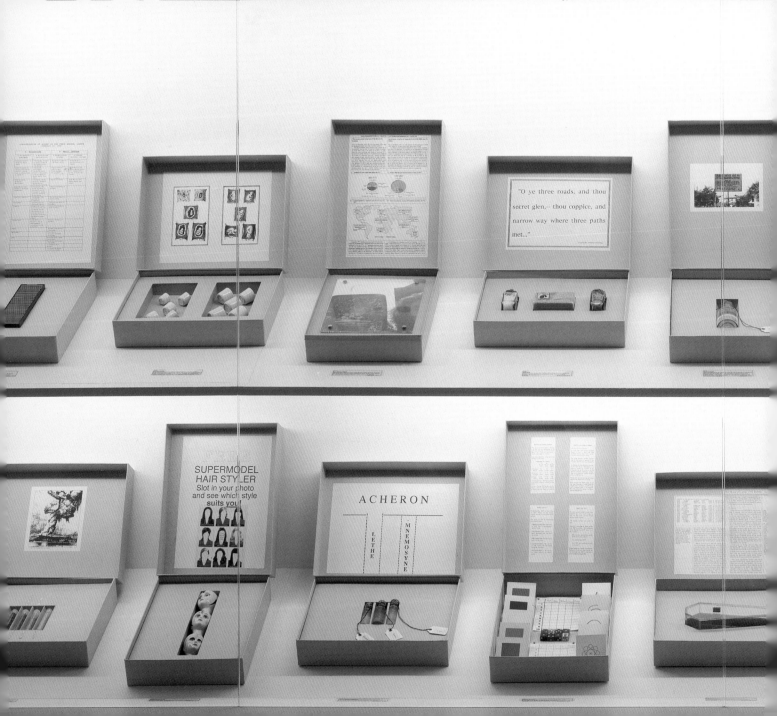

"O ye three roads, and thou secret glen,-- thou coppice, and narrow way where three paths met..."

SUPERMODEL HAIR STYLER
Slot in your photo and see which style suits you!

ACHERON

LETHE

MNEMOSYNE

I PRESENT
WORLD RECORD
ARTISTIC

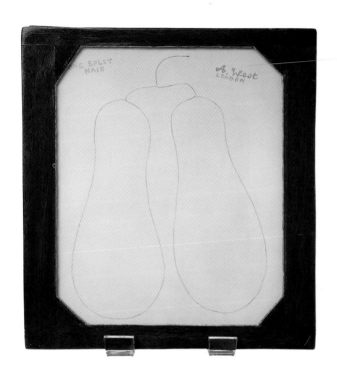

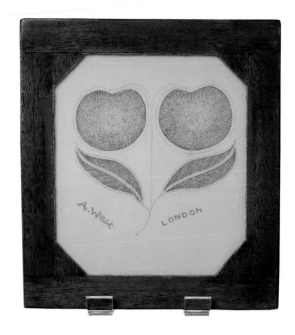

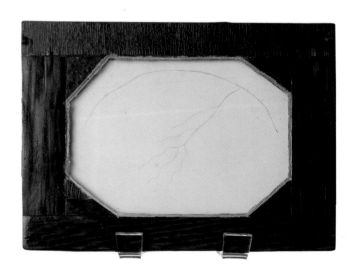

43   [OPPOSITE]

Split Hairs: The Art of Alfie West

1998, details

44

Split Hairs: The Art of Alfie West

1998, details of reverse

Anamorphosis of the Gaze

Stella Santacatterina

45

Wild Talents 1997
Galeria Foksal, Warsaw 1997

Anamorphosis of the Gaze

Stella Santacatterina

*Muses are like women who slip out during the night when no one is looking and give
themselves to unknown sailors, then return and speak about Chinese porcelain.* w.b. yeats

Susan Hiller's work occupies an original and anticipatory place with respect to the landscape
of contemporary international art, drawing on many cultural references, from anthropology
to psychoanalysis to mass media technologies, and operating across various means from
photography to installation, sound and object. It presents a continuity of aesthetic experience
that the artist began in the early 1970s through an exploration of the deep place of visibility
using complex and poetic minimal means. Marcel Proust might have said that her work is
an astonishing revelation of the 'mysterious phenomenon of scintillation'. It searches at
one and the same time for the secret source of artistic creation and the place of its realisation.

Hiller's work pays particular attention to the way vision is connected to the dynamics
of remembrance, knowledge, imagination and dream, with all the signs of the unconscious
and the archetypes of collective memory. If the phenomenological world is a catalogue of
statistics, the fantasy of the artist confronts the false surface of appearances to insert the
invisible, exorbitant energies of the imagination and touch the poles of the disturbing and
amazing. The imagination, says Foucault, is not in fact the way of reality; instead it is the realm
of the actual, a means to traverse obliquely concrete presence in order to make emerge the
primal dimension. In this respect all her work is 'work in progress', a circular interrogation
which oscillates between the presence of the question and the absence of the answer.

Psi Girls, first exhibited in 1999, is an installation of five simultaneous video projections,
each a montage of brief sequences from various popular films that figure an act of telekinesis
performed by young girls. For instance, among them we recognise the sequences in which,
through her powers of concentration alone, a girl spins a pencil on its point (Andrew Fleming's
The Craft, 1996), or accelerates a miniature train around a track (Brian De Palma's *The Fury*,
1978), or shifts glasses across a table to smash out of frame onto the floor (Andrei Tarkovsky's
Stalker, 1979). Each screen is suffused by a different colour, altering the nature of the images
and remapping their semantic meanings: violet and the sacred, green and the supernatural,
blue and regeneration, yellow and transgression, red and passion. Of the six primary colours,
orange, thought by psychologists to reflect internal harmony, is 'missing'. The projections are
accompanied by a pulsating soundtrack remixed from a gospel choir, which contributes to a
sense of disorientation and amazement. Roger Caillois speaks of such disorientation as linking
'the sense of vertigo and the pleasure to destroy order and stability.'' Indeed Hiller's work is
always orchestrated around nuances of the occult and aberrant, the play of the vertiginous,
and a ludic panic that produces a disjunction with established reality.

This disjunction is both external to the work, in its relation to the viewer, and internal, in its choice of themes. *Wild Talents*, 1997, juxtaposes documentary footage about a miraculous visionary appearance and religious pilgrimage with the destructive psychokinetic power of children as projected through the images of mass media. This destruction of order is accentuated by the soundtrack of breaking objects, so that what is witnessed by the spectator has a double value: on the one hand it is understood as a representation, but on the other it is experienced as real. As in *Psi Girls*, Hiller creates a journey that activates a dynamic that works to defeat any certainty of the visible, developing an intentional disequilibrium of knowledge. In this respect, the artist operates a kind of language parallel to science where she manipulates suspicion and doubt to pass beyond established conventions. Her work deals with a phantasmatic internal world, but this world relies also, in Hegelian terms, on a series of transformations, which are able to exteriorise the work. Hiller's work needs and is nourished by ghosts, but at the same time gives itself through a work of transformation in which potential meanings multiply and constantly shift into other possible constructions.

All Hiller's artistic practice is crossed and penetrated by memory and nostalgia; representations of images that are distant, lost or denied, which emerge from oblivion. Like the historical example of the Surrealists, the concept of mourning in Hiller's work affirms itself almost as an intrinsic quality of the language of art itself. And yet nostalgia for the lost disorder underlines the new order of form. It is born from conscious awareness of art and of its contrary, the unconscious; in other words, born from the ambivalence of each gesture, because it is exactly ambivalence that gives the gesture a real affect through the presence in it of vital affirmation and mortal negation. There is no nostalgia, in fact, that is not remembrance; the myth of Mnemosyne can stand for both memory and nostalgia. Mnemosyne is the daughter of sky and earth, of Uranus and Gaia, in other words, the daughter of the visible and the invisible, from the past and the present. The birth of Mnemosyne challenges a spatial and temporal limit. The language of art is always marked by this presence; the link of art with memory is not therefore a casual relation but is inscribed in its roots, in its essence. Nostalgia, when it becomes the language of art, always elaborates itself as ambivalence, as also does memory, producing an image that always comes back from a distant time and place, a movement of thought towards what is behind, lost, discarded – a distance that breaks the rules of the irreversible and impossible.

In both *Wild Talents* and *Psi Girls* the artist's mode of operation is similar to the analytic aesthetic of Godard, who constructed a mechanism capable of triggering the self-reflective and critical aspect of the filmic as well as the televisual image. His process was to slow down and deconstruct the flux of the image and treat each frame as if it were a photographic image. Especially in *Psi Girls*, where the artist uses five monitors, the new narrative shifts temporality from the linearity and succession of conventional film to the direct immediacy of the event more typical of TV, or even theatre. We are still voyeurs, but we are captured by the moment.

Hiller understands that the photographic image, despite its privilege as a seemingly pure registering of the material world, is nonetheless an oblique eye capable of reflecting things but in a modified way. *From India to the Planet Mars*, a series of illuminated photo-transparencies of obscure calligraphies, takes its title from a book by Theodore Flournoy (Switzerland, 1899) based on messages written automatically by Helen Smith, which, according to her, represented the language of Mars and India. Hiller's drawings derive from not only the artist herself but also other sources (students and friends as well as Victor Hugo, George Yeats, the analysands of Dr Anita Muhl and Frederick Bligh Bond). This is also a work in progress, in which the transparencies take on the qualities of both drawing and photograph, and where the illuminated gesture refers back to the experience of writing itself. But it is a deceptive linguistic process, a displacement from drawing to positive to negative transparency, whose deep meaning lies in its reference to an action that has already happened but which alludes to the real experience of the artist. It is the awareness of a subject that controls the flow of time and her own individual presence, but that also enables the viewer to recompose the work by connecting his or her own individual memory and experience in time. As in most of Hiller's works, *From India to the Planet Mars,* alludes to the possibility of a journey, which is nostalgic not in the sense of a regressive return, but rather of the elastic capacity of memory for infinite extension.

Dream Screens, 1996, is a work designed for late-night web-browsers (to be found on the Dia Center's website). It is constructed around the artists' colour wheel (here in the form of a web), dissolving fields of colour and a collection of whispered narratives based on dreams articulated against three background sounds: pulsar, Morse code and heartbeat. Light and energy are amongst the greatest mysteries of our time and colour has much to do with this, since it permeates everything. Colour – extremely mobile, gradable – comes, like the pulsar, from the furthest place, which is also the unthinkable. This infinite distance between subject and object is the original place from which aesthetic sensibility emerges.

As Nietzsche commented, 'we need all the petulant, fluctuating, dancing, derisive, childlike and beatific air in order not to lose the freedom over things that are idealistically demanded from us.' Freedom is not a value outside temporality, but rather a continuous, tangential meeting with the world that happens outside the symmetrical movement of reason. Imagination here is neither conceived as an onanistic exercise on the possibility of the world nor as an allegorical emphasis on the simple interiority of the artist, but as an integral functionality uncontaminated by exteriority. From here, the intriguing and uncanny images the artist produces are founded in an optical play of anamorphosis, a perspective construction that makes strange things happen magically, pushing narrative meaning towards paradox and contradiction. As with the anamorphic figure in Holbein's painting *The Ambassadors,* the gaze carries a warning that disorder comes from order, and that a tormented world can result from the most rigorous organisation. Anamorphosis is a mechanical process, the logical but deformed consequence of perspectival optics, and links with the cold technological media Hiller uses. In her work the fertile zone is the margin.

Fully aware of the irremediable linguistic nature of art, the artist articulates her work from this margin. This means that the work moves around the web of the imagination beyond the narrow confines of the psychology of the subject. Hiller's images carry the memory of the imagination itself, but as with language, the imagination must go beyond the self to belong fully to contemporaneity. Furthermore, this artistic attitude confirms a will to create a change within artistic structure, but above all a revolution at the level of art's meaning, to take into account an external referent, expressing a need for history and action as well as fantasy (and in this sense Hiller is a 'European' artist). In her case we can speak about art as a double gaze: one is external, incorporating the image of the world whilst transforming it; the other is an act of deviation, a transverse and circular practice belonging to fantasy. This fantastic activity can neither be influenced by the symbolic decodification of psychoanalysis nor by a search for motivation in the artist's ego, but is an imagination that projects itself to the exterior in order to transform it.

Hiller's practice is a revitalisation of creativity that links both to the imagination and the irrational and functions as a singular critique of both our culture and art. If we consider the condition of contemporary aesthetic research where there is a tendency to privilege the rational and the material over the spiritual, magical and mythic, Hiller's work demonstrates the necessity of art to rescue aspects of the mythopoietic, the imagination and the irrational. This does not mean to go against reason, but rather to recuperate mythic possibility. Therefore her attitude is different to that of the Surrealists since, although she cultivates the occult and oneiric, it is never for the dream in itself. Her artistic practice realises not so much objects as conceptual journeys in which the viewer can once again travel on a journey which is always exercised within the boundary of ritual to confirm, traced through image, sound and words to confirm a field of absolute knowledge.

The experience of automatic writing, in Hiller's work, which first appeared in *Sisters of Menon*, 1972, and continues through *From India to the Planet Mars* and the telekinetic powers described in *Psi Girls*, is very close to Blanchot's idea of writing, where art is an adventure in which the artist loses herself. Art is a space deprived of subjectivity: to draw, to write, demands the evacuation of the ego because only when the world becomes invisible can be born the event of art. For Blanchot, 'blindness is the poetic space of vision'[2]; for Heidegger, for a work of art to be 'successful' it must completely negate the person and the name of the poet, evoking the spoken in its pure state. In other words, the object of art is without subject.

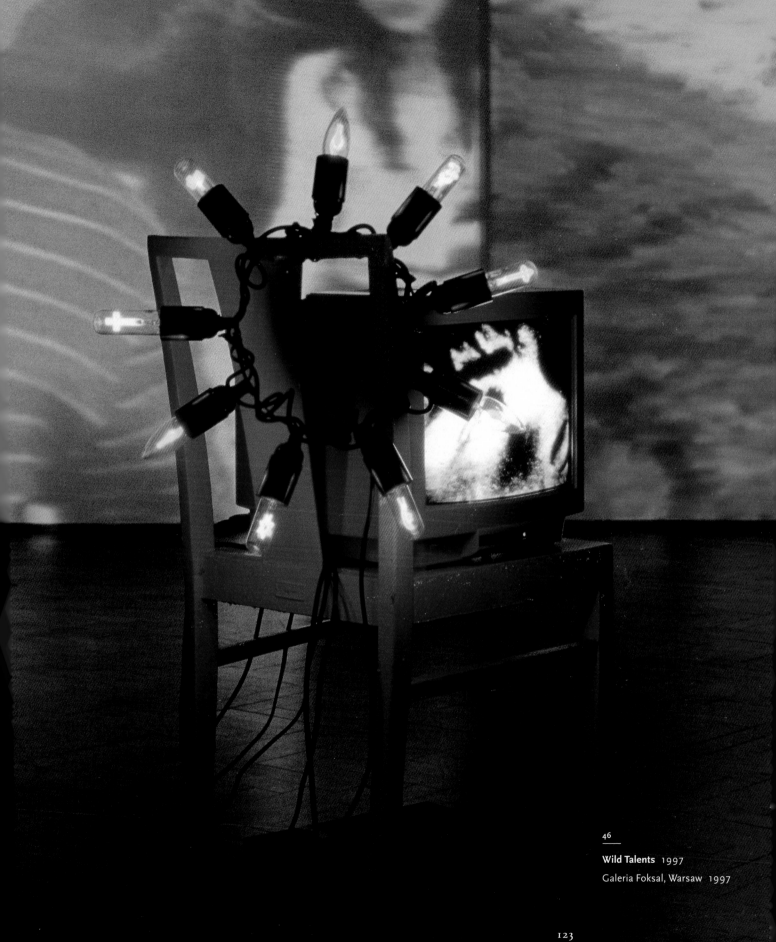

46
Wild Talents 1997
Galeria Foksal, Warsaw 1997

47
___

Wild Talents 1997
Experimental Art Foundation,
Adelaide 1998

When we grow older and wiser
We learn, with perhaps a little regret,
That these things can never be.

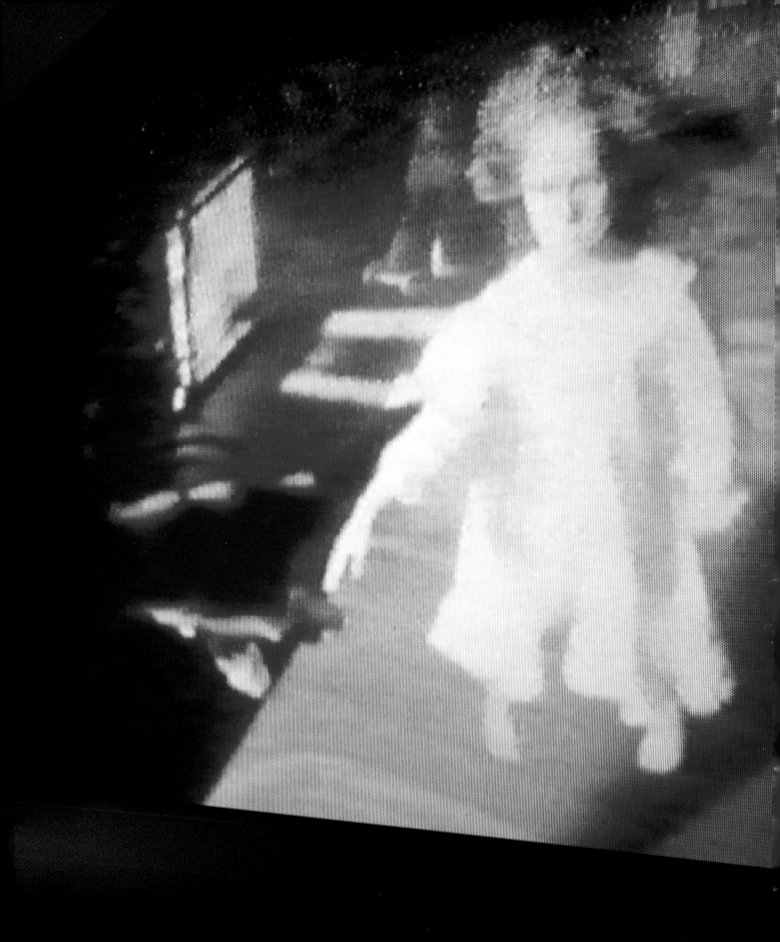

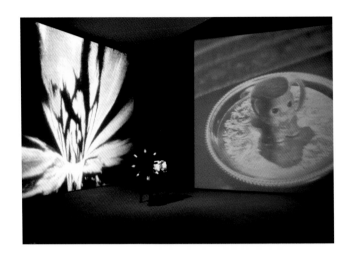

48

Psi Girls 1999
Gagosian Gallery, New York 2001

49

Psi Girls 1999

Delfina Gallery, London 1999

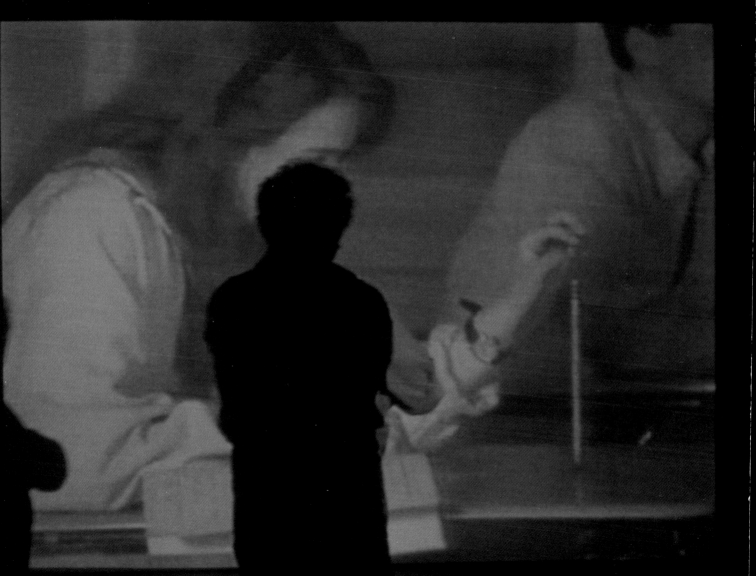

3. PRECOGNITION

4. PSYCHIC

5. TELEKINESIS or
PSYCHOKINESIS

...knowledge of a future event.

One possessing mental abilities that defy scientific knowledge

he ability to move objects by thought alone

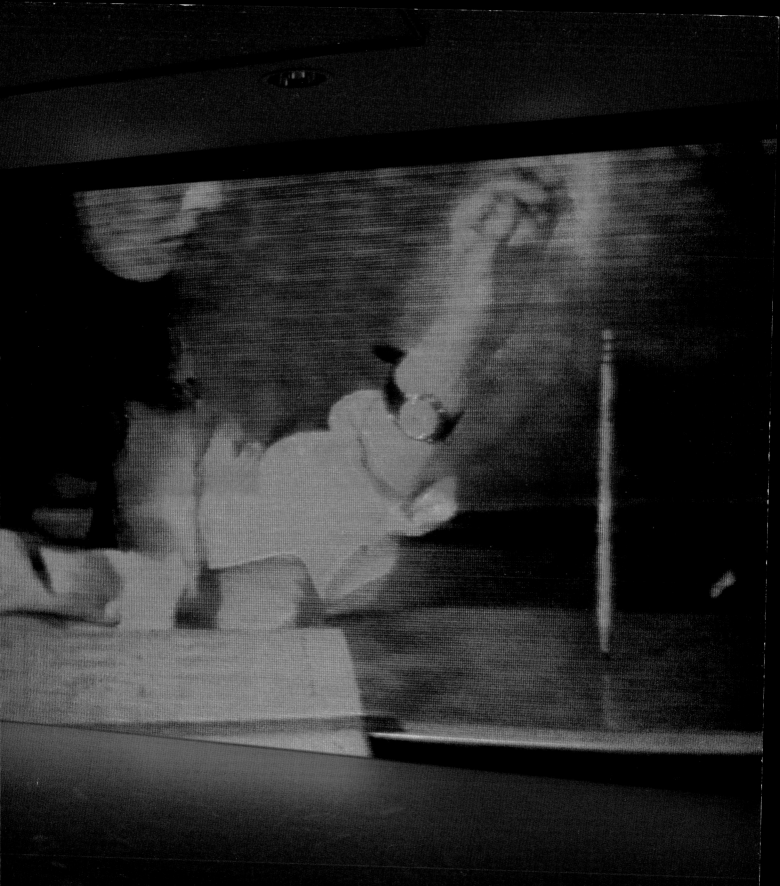

On the Side of the Angels

Louise Milne

50

Witness 2000

detail

On the Side of the Angels
Witness and Other Works

Louise Milne

Susan Hiller's *Witness* (2000) is experienced as an unfolding topology. The installation is first seen through the frame of its entrance: an open forest of silvery wires and dangling ovoids, filling the top half of a room. A dim, faintly perceptible sussuration emanates from the space. There may be people inside, causing waves in the fronds, or standing slightly bent, hand to head. A few steps in, the environment clarifies further: the "forest" is made of flat round speakers, like microphones or radios, each hanging at the end of its speaker wire. The denser stratum of the oval speakers forms a thick, complex horizon, like a printer's matrix. These irregular endpoints delineate the variable band of human ear-height (from walking children to the very tall). The interface between the lower void of the room and its upper striations thus takes the shape of a formalised wavy sea – an impression reinforced by the whispering ambient sound. We are inside a kind of *mappa mundi*; a map or image of the world. This takes seconds to apprehend somatically, the body instantly reaching for the relevant analogies.

The fourth dimension, time, the medium of this interaction, is further complicated when the visitor fully enters and explores the grove of wires. One first chooses and grasps a single speaker, and holds it to the ear. Each speaker produces a different result at a different time. Inviting this action, Hiller choreographs together the experiences of plucking a fruit, smelling a flower, holding a conch shell to "hear the sea", or tuning a radio.

Every speaker transmits a voice telling a story. The voices speak in a great range of languages; eventually, one realises that they are all relating stories of close encounters with UFOs (Unidentified Flying Objects), or Flying Saucers. Before examining these testimonies – and Hiller's orchestration of them – in more detail, consider the range of positions available to the listener with which to categorise this late 20 c phenomenon: UFO sightings. They may be fictional, illusory or hallucinatory (a somewhat different category); or physically real. If the latter, they may be interpreted as man-made, natural, extra-terrestrial or supernatural.

Accounts of moving lights in the sky have a long history in the west, as elsewhere. C. G. Jung argued in 1959 that the (then) current epidemic of UFO sightings, the first of its kind, should be interpreted as a genuine spate of visions: new clothing for a very old type of psycho-religious experience. Jung commented that "spontaneous psychic phenomena" of this kind are well-attested in the experience of hermits, who could evaluate such "numinous fantasy images" either positively or negatively. Many, though by no means all, of the experiences related in *Witness* happened to people while they were outside the social world – on their own, at night, in transit along a country road, by a lake or river, or crossing a desert.

Anyone can see how great the work is, on attempting to fit language into visions, visions in which these things which are united in nature are separated, and things separated in nature are united... It is no mean achievement to pass on to another something of a strange nature that has stirred in one's own soul, for [by] this phantasy things which are expelled from the order of being, and things which never in any possible way existed, are brought instead into being – nay, even things which have not a nature capable of existence.∴
Synesius of Cyrene (d. 412 AD)[1]

vulgar minds (?)... have heard of horses of fire and chariots of fire appearing in the sky, described and doubtless perceived with such distinctness that the listener almost imagines he too beholds the movements of embattled hosts upon the plains of heaven.
Dr Moore (1855)[2]

Today... men pay an extraordinary amount of attention to the skies, for technological reasons. This is especially true of the airman [pilot], whose field of vision is occupied on the one hand by the complicated control apparatus before him, and on the other by the empty vastness of cosmic space. His consciousness is concentrated one-sidedly on details requiring the most careful observation, while at his back, so to speak, his consciousness strives to fill the illimitable emptiness of space.
C. G. Jung (1959)[3]

Panic dissolves the bonds of a little society, characterized by a high degree of reinforcement and involution, placed as it is outside the territory proper to the city.. [It] thus typically attacks a model of order and disrupts it.
Philippe Borgeaud (1988) [4]

Consider the classical account of panic, understood as an attack by the god Pan. Longus described such "Pan-ic" visions as a disordering of the senses:
On a sudden all the land seemed to be on fire; then anon their ears were struck with an impetuous clattering of oars as if a great navy were coming... here some thought they must be wounded, there others lay like dead men. A man would have thought he had seen a kind of nocturnal battle, when yet there was no enemy there.[5]

Compare these testimonies in *Witness*:
I was glowing. Everything was glowing... It was a marvel. [track 11] [6]
... it landed on the roof of the car... the heat was intense. Our hair was standing straight up and we felt... like we were being dehydrated. It was awful, frightening, like our brains were being sucked out. My fear was that I would be pulled out of my body. I put my hand out of the window and touched something spongy that burnt my hand. I thought that we were going to die. [03.20, text]

The aesthetic effect of listening to these voices, in the forest of speakers, has little to do with our categories – fact or fiction – for the evidence of UFO sightings. Whatever we think about these things, the testimonies confront us directly with their ancestral category: the experience of the fantastic, defined by Todorov as "hesitation". This sense of hovering on a threshold, unable to choose between competing sets of contexts, strongly characterises our response to these stories: the feeling that "*I nearly reached the point of believing...*" Roger Caillois, the theorist of play, situates this effect more plainly in the world of signs, evoking Foucault's *Order of Things*: *The fantastic is always a break in the acknowledged order, an irruption of the inadmissable within a changeless everyday reality.*[8]

The fantastic is that hesitation experienced by a person who knows only the laws of nature, confronting an apparently supernatural event.
Tzvetan Todorov (1970) [7]

Many of the witnesses speak of this sense of rupture (*I rubbed my eyes in disbelief... I thought we were dreaming*). The impact of such "breaks" in reality may be often highly emotional. Jung describes a typical "roller-coaster" transition, from fear or apprehension at the start of the vision to ecstasy, awe or calm at its centre. These emotions appear in the testimonies; terror and shock are most often reported, but the coloured lights of the object are often described as beautiful, and many describe a sense of cosmic wonder:
He told me he was "asphyxiated with fear" [Zimbabwe, 01.12]
I was so frightened that I have blocked out some of my memory of the sighting [USA, track 6]
I was so shocked, I felt out of my mind [Japan, 02.01]
We felt as if we could not move or speak, because we were so shocked by the sight
[Papua New Guinea, 03.24]
I still have the scar on my face to this day. Whenever I touch it I feel a tingling sensation and I experience a wonderful feeling of oneness, of unity with the earth itself [Sweden, 04.25]
I felt afraid, but not a normal fear, more like a sense of awe [Brazil, 07.16]
It was the greatest joy I have ever known. I felt a cosmic consciousness [Sweden, 04.26]
This incident revealed something rare and inexplicable [Uruguay, 08.26]
It was absolutely awe-inspiring to see it... such a beautiful-looking thing [UK, 09.23]

A sense of release at a moment of change in everyday reality is in itself not mysterious. The mind has evolved to require (and accommodate) such breaks from consciousness. They occur involuntarily, everyday in sleep, and are consciously sought after in the varieties of ecstatic experience: religious, aesthetic, sexual. These all climax in the end of desire, the little death. All involve a hiatus of the ego. The "text of the self" is suspended, producing a release from oppressive self-consciousness. This loss of self is often characterised by the release of a flood of emotion – perceived as positive or negative *jouissance* – depending on whether the subject embraces or fears the experience.

When the Greek diarist Aristides describes a close encounter with Asklepios, god of healing, his own religion, pursued over many years, provides him with the "script" for this meeting. Even so, when the encounter arrives, its physical markers are those we now associate more with terror; he is literally beside himself.

As with sleep, as one emerges from the hiatus, one must fabricate some account of where the self has been. This explains several points about the structuring of the testimonies in *Witness*. The returning ego must write itself back into being; more precisely, it writes itself in retroactively, over the space in the immediate past where it lay in hiatus. In so doing, it manufactures a kind of memory, a dream-experience, a "holding fantasy" which effectively sutures together the edges of the break in consciousness. The dream can thus be thought of as a repair, or darn, to the ego; producing "wrinkles" in reality around the repair. Traditionally, dream-experience identified itself as dream, through the fantasy conventions used to enact the suture: transformations of scale, of colour, impossibly hybrid things, reversals and displacements. Many of these elements appear in the *Witness* stories: incredible movements, weird colours, shape-shifting machines and alien variations on the human form. The presence of "typed" elements of fantasy is especially clear in stories of encounters with aliens, which may begin like dreams (*I was lying in bed...* [05.38; 10.12; 10.13]), or resemble older tales of visits with elves or "little people" (*They took me to a huge pavilion where couples were dancing* [09.17; 09.24]).

More sinister motifs to do with penetrating the skin, breaking and re-ordering the body, also have pre-industrial ancestors. For example, in old Siberia, candidates for the role of shaman, were represented as experiencing ceremonial dismemberment. Compare the activities of the alien *Mutende-ya-ngenge*, which "*sometimes captures human beings, cuts them open, then closes them up again and makes them forget what happened*" [Africa, 01.04] with legends recorded in the eleventh-century by the demonologist, Gervasius of Tilburg: *[There are] men and women who fly about at night, penetrating the skins of fellow mortals and oppressing them whilst they sleep [with] nightmares... [they also] break the legs of slumbering mortals and then put them together again...*"

Such motifs acknowledge a fundamental principle in the construction of dreams and visions. When the ego undergoes hiatus, the virtual experience is remembered in a fragmentary or partial way. There is no such thing as a "whole" dream. The dream-memory always seems like part of a greater whole, the rest of which has been lost (compare the parallel illusion of "completeness" associated with waking consciousness). In fact, this fragmentary perception is to do with the necessary conditions of (re-)writing the ego back into the world. However, there are wider implications here, realised in Hiller's installations, about the nature of waking visions, and their atmosphere of inexplicable mystery.

[All] was revealed in the clearest possible way... For I seemed almost to touch him and to perceive that he himself was coming, and to be halfway between sleep and waking and to want to get the power of vision and to be anxious lest he depart beforehand, and to have turned my ears to listen, sometimes as in a dream, sometimes as in a waking vision, and my hair was standing on end and tears of joy [came forth], and the weight of knowledge was no burden – what man could even describe these things in words? But if he is one of the initiates, then he knows and understands.
Aelius Aristides (c. 129–179 AD) [9]

The candidate's limbs are removed and disjointed with an iron hook; the bones are cleaned, the flesh scraped, the body fluids thrown away, and the eyes torn from their sockets. After this operation all the bones are gathered up and fastened together with iron... His bones are then covered with new flesh, and in some cases he is also given new blood.
G. V. Ksenofontov (1955) [10]

In dreaming, the distortions around the suture are usually clear: no culture mistakes dreaming and waking experience, though, of course, they may be valued and assessed quite differently, as equivalent realities or as totally disconnected. But in the case of the waking vision, the witness is naturally convinced of its reality, and must convey this in the fabric of the story. The witnesses therefore represent the U F O sightings as real and fantastic *at the same time*; the rupture is located in the world, and so the suture must also be located there. Hence the nearly universal use of rationalist narrative as a framing device firmly to locate the event – and the listener – in a specific place and time: *it was shortly before 23.00 on February 15th, 1994... on Tuesday December 10th, at 7.20 in the evening... By 2.30am, we were in the Nullabor Plain... At a point six miles from the shore of Nagasaki Prefecture...*

We are now close upon the Norwegian coast – in the sixth-eighth degree of latitude... It is now within a few days of three years since what I am going to tell you occurred. It was on the tenth of July, 18___
Edgar Allan Poe, *Descent into the Maelstrom* (1841)

This exactitude about details recalls the conventions of the classic realist novel, the scientific or news report, the police statement, and, of course, testimony in a court of law; allusions present in the many connotations of the word, *witness*, whose oldest religious sense was "to be present at a marvel".[12] Realist framing devices have been applied since the nineteenth-century to fictional and factual accounts of the paranormal. Edgar Allan Poe pioneered this technique in his classic tales of horror.

Like earlier witnesses of ghosts and phantoms, Hiller's informants supply their names, ages, occupations, and geographical and temporal coordinates. They name other witnesses. Some assert their sobriety. Their scene-setting starts with details apparently tangential to the main drama, but which are actually essential corroborative elements in building a secure "bridge", rooted in mundane reality, into, and then away from, the rupture itself.

I now feel I have reached a point of this narrative at which every reader will be startled into positive disbelief. It is my business, however, simply to proceed.
Edgar Allan Poe, *The Facts in the Case of M. Valdemar* (1845)

Then comes the point of suture, and the point of resemblance to the fragmentary nature of the dream. Oneiric (i.e. dreamlike) fragmentation in these visions presents itself in terms of enigma and mystery attached to the *absent part of the history* of the object itself. Each phenomenon is described as inexplicable on several levels: its behaviour, its arrival and departure, its physics and chemistry, its visual appearance (veering between mechanical, organic or celestial), but it is also seen as a kind of clue, and so recognised as partial. In short, the witnesses testify to a lack, a missing mechanism, or withheld portion of narrative, that would somehow enable them to make better sense of the experience. Many of those who put their stories on the internet, end their narratives by asking for an explanation, or failing that, a fellow witness. At the same time, paradoxically, the power of these exact descriptions of the fantastic resides in the fact that no "rational" explanation can be forthcoming: the enigma at the centre is held open, and most of the stories conclude as they started, with a step-by-step bridge back into the mundane.

I know that this was something very real and very important.
[China, 02.20]

Turning from the components of the installation to its significance as a whole work, as Hiller herself comments, at the end of her notes on the *Witness* files: *What's coming through these voices is far richer than the subject matter of their stories...*[13] The whole is indeed greater than the sum of its parts, for Hiller's art is "collective" in every sense of the word. Here, as has been her longstanding practice, ingredients are chosen and collected with an unerring eye for their secret possibilities, then expertly choreographed into something entirely new and unexpected. Wonder and revelation, as well as analyses of these states, lie at the heart of this art.

The effect of the testimonies *en masse*, arranged into a giant polyphony of "nonsense music" in the original languages, transforms the individual accounts by changing the stresses between these key aspects: the "corroborative" rationalist framing, hesitation in the face of the fantastic, emotional engagement, and the sense of oneiric or fragmentary perception. The listener in *Witness* instead receives a primary impression of wholeness, because the work makes manifest the global range, breadth and intensity of such visions. The work asserts the continuing validity of visionary experience as an inherent faculty of mind, irrespective of its science-fictional or scientific costume. The "occult dimension" – meaning that which is hidden or invisible – is revealed as an active social and psychic category, a site central to the experience of art.

Alfred Gell defined the occult as: *the place where things are when they are not happening*,[15] and clearly UFOs belong in this dimension, emerging magically from it to disrupt our own, and returning to it just as mysteriously. However, it would be equally true to say that the occult is the proper home less for the UFO itself than for its *missing explanation*; that presumed explanation whose absence tugs so persistently at the witnesses. If the occult is where the UFOs and aliens are "when they are not happening", then this is where the unavailable part of their narrative must be also. This will be the case no matter what genre of explanation we envisage: whether the visitors are technologically superior aliens from Orion, angels, humans or devils.

In the context of the installation, *Witness*, the pattern of "lack" at the heart of each account is literally trans-figured by being lifted into the self-contained parameters of the work of art. *Witness* provides its *own* occult dimension: the hundreds of voices are perceptibly present, in the "same" space as the single enigmatic account, speaking in one's ear. Both become part of the consciousness of the listener, whose active participation, and serial attention to these complexly fragmented testimonies, sets up a mobile field which transcends individual lack. We could say instead that it is the listener's awareness which apprehends this lack as narrative desire, moving ceaselessly through the piece, and so generating pleasure. What Barthes would call a "wavy meaning" is produced – *jouissance* set off like a string of firecrackers in the head.

Formally, one theme that emerges is the artist's interest in the necessary tension inherent in oneiric suture – the effort of holding together the edges of two different realities – and the hesitation at the heart of our experience of the fantastic – predicated on the opposite realisation that it is not possible to bring these edges completely together. The seam will always show, however consciousness tries to stitch it, but the seam is also a doorway into the suspended space of the fantastic, and therefore to be prized as a means of release, whether it is seen as a path to the sublime (a complete absence of figuration), or as liberation into the repertoire of dreams (absolute figuration).

The cultural symbols of occult power... Gods and spirits, or disembodied magical influences such as mana, cannot be considered the occult order per se, but are only images of it. Being products of the human mind, they are knowable absolutely, while it is of the essence of the occult that it is not known, that it cannot be grasped in itself.

In positing any array of spirits, powers and mystical forces, men create an imaginary world to which they, as its originators, have privileged access. A spirit is not and cannot be an unknown quantity because, as a spirit, it is a figment of human thought processes; it exists only inasmuch as it is known... the spirit [is] the knowable image or representation of something that is in its essence unknowable. Alfred Gell (1974) [14]

The [work] is varied through a certain number of substitute objects standing in a strict relationship to [each other]: they are similar (since they are all spherical) and at the same time dissimilar (they are all [calling] something different)... [These] substitutes are declined in every sense of the word; revealed like states of the one identity; offered like propositions none of which can hold more meaning than another, filled out like successive moments in the story. Roland Barthes (1963) [16]

If you look at any walls spotted with various stains... you will be able to see in it a resemblance [to] different landscapes adorned with mountains, rivers, rocks, trees, plains, wide valleys [and] hills. You will also be able to see divers combats and figures in quick movement, and strange expressions of faces, and outlandish costumes, and an infinite number of things, which you can then reduce into separate and well-conceived forms. With such walls... it comes about as it does with the sound of bells, in whose clanging you may discover every name and word that you can imagine.
Leonardo da Vinci (c.1490) [17]

I saw myself in a world of light. Mountains and deserts were a rainbow of colored light, red, yellow, white, blue. I experienced an overwhelming nostalgia for them. I became as though struck by madness and was carried outside myself by the violence of the presence and the deep emotion I experienced...
Shamsoddin Lhaiji (15th c), quoted in Susan Hiller, Dream Screens (1996) [18]

Civilisation regulates the transition [in humans] from one [mental] state to another. Thanks to art, the multiple states of the human being must, in spite of everything, become livable possibilities. The only reality in art is furnished by the hallucinatory experience... We were determined to become one with our hallucinations.
Jean-Jacques Lebel (1966) [19]

In experiences which appear to be partly hallucinatory, the subject's environment may actually be entirely hallucinatory, even when the subject reports no obvious reason for suggesting this to be so. Celia Green (1975) [20]

This concern is common to several of Hiller's earlier works; notably *Belshazzar's Feast* (1984), *Magic Lantern* (1987), *Bright Shadow* (1994) and *Dream Screens* (1996). Each presents a situation wherein the spectator is invited to make images from ambiguous visual or aural cues, unfurling over time. Such pieces investigate the mind's capacity to see a pattern, to doubt that it sees it, and to be fascinated by this movement. Hiller's web-based piece, *Dream Screens*, consists of eighty-four separate colour fields, to be changed at will by the viewer, in any order. This is accompanied by a complex soundtrack, which interleaves spoken passages, loosely based on memories of films, all of which have the word *dream* in their titles. The sound fades in with a statement in Morse code: "I am dreaming". Then Hiller's voice relates the plots from the films as if they were her own experiences. Or the viewer may decide to hear other women's voices, narrating the text in Japanese, French, Russian, German or Spanish. The "drum-beat" pattern of the Morse code fades out, and turns into another rhythm, a pulsar signal, from a far galaxy. The voice tells more film-stories; the pulsar gives way to a human heart-beat... Woven into all this are other pieces of spoken text, drawn from ancient and modern meditations on the nature of dreams and dreaming.

The result is a kind of matrix, navigated by a shifting first person. This strange "I" moves as if in a fragmented dream, through a remembered cinematic "multiverse", whose extremes are designated by changes in scale and code; from the microcosmic ("brainwaves") to the cosmic (pulsar); from the meta-fictional to the somatic (heart-beat). Another web-page shows the colours as a map of the site, around a diagrammatic wheel or web, like a medieval map with Jerusalem at the centre. Below, the names of the colours, listed in columns, generate a Poundian *poesis*; *Venetian Red, Dragon's Blood, Saffron, Bremen Blue.* The concrete history of "colour-in-the-world" is concentrated into this array of names, weightless on the screen, elegantly suggesting the ancient global geographies of trade and manufacture. The viewer realises that the apparently fixed visual spectrum of colours and names contains unexamined layers of fantasy, artifice and metaphor. As one explores this shifting web of sounds and memories, the colours and their associative powers work hypnogogically, stretching and releasing relations between eyes, ears, memory and place.

This kind of investigation into changes of state is central to Hiller's sister installations, *Wild Talents* (1997) and *Psi Girls* (1999). As in *Witness*, these are multi-media environments which unlock and expand the meaning of found sources: here, moments of paranormal imagery from late 20th century Western cinema, sourced and reworked by Hiller. The clips have been edited, looped, extended, unified with colour filters, magnified and bent around two huge screens (*Wild Talents*), or sequenced rhythmically over five screens (*Psi Girls*). Like *Dream Screens*, each has a complex soundtrack acting as commentary and frame. The repeating sequences of *Psi Girls* are accompanied by ecstatic gospel clapping, and end with a burst of white noise. *Wild Talents* includes intoned voice-overs, visual texts, and a separate visual commentary: part of a documentary showing children (visibly) experiencing (invisible) religious visions. This runs simultaneously on a small television, standing in the installation space, festooned with religious fairy lights.

Hiller's background materials for these pieces include research on two distinct historical figures, whose careers and ideas subliminally inform the meaning of the works. Her titles come from Charles Fort's last book, *Wild Talents* (1932),[22] and his vision of a future where *Psi Girls* do battle. The second figure is the Polish psychic Stefan Ossowiecki (d. 1944), who harnessed his initially chaotic childhood "wild talents" into an ability to find lost objects and people.[23] Their lives demonstrate how technological society has re-constructed the human paranormal and recuperated the waking fantastic. Such cultural metamorphoses are the deeper subjects of *Wild Talents* and *Psi Girls* (as they are for *Witness*). The viewer's first point of entry to this real subject-matter is to do with Hiller's re-framing of the visual conventions peculiar to contemporary cinema.

The *prima materia* for each work is the selection of film-clips. These all use the "magic" of cinema to show young people demonstrating uncanny or paranormal powers: telekinesis, levitation, the animation of inanimate objects. Hiller finds unexpected significance embedded in this material, as in *Witness*. Where the testimonies in *Witness* used rationalist corroborative detail to frame their occult matter, the equivalent in the film-clips is the realist *mise-en-scène* of cinematic narrative. The original film-makers engaged in one kind of "stitching", to erase the "strings" around the magical or impossible action (the glass pulled off the table, the hidden flame under the boiling cocoa, etc.), by which we might see the trick being done. In this way, scenes of magic are represented as apparently seamless, and so surreal, collages of the real and unreal.

In a surreal still image such as a painting, the surreality depends on what the viewer perceives as missing connections between the anomalous elements. Hence the sense of mystery such images evoke, as with the "missing" explanations of the UFOs. But in a work of surreal cinema, the audience does not experience this bafflement, because we are well aware that whole teams of people are at work behind the camera to produce the effect. Special effects of this kind have become a particular category of *jouissance* in their own right, precisely because of the release they offer into acknowledgement of artifice, a kind of collapse of the suspension of disbelief. Hiller herself has called them "moments of pleasure."[25] Todorovian "hesitation" in the face of the fantastic becomes speculation about the exact nature of the conjuring. By removing each piece of magic from its original narrative framework, Hiller restores this suspension, and so creates a hallucinatory focus.

The elements of *Psi Girls*, for example, appear now as a set of mythemes:[27] each a constellation, a term in the same series. The orchestration of the five "terms" – like balanced units in a looped musical phrase – means we no longer see their individual impossibilities in terms of the parent movie genre (horror or otherwise).[28] The kind of transformative re-alignment accomplished in *Witness* through the play with scale is here achieved through strategies of repetition and dissociation.

Our apprehension of the repressed artifice – the conjured relationship between the real and imaginary in each quoted scene – begins to change. Just as the rationalist bracketing of the accounts in *Witness* is transmuted into a common sense of wonder, so the realist *mise-en-scène* of cinema is eclipsed, and so transcended, in *Wild Talents* and *Psi Girls*. We no longer perceive the suturing in the scenes from a film-going audience's viewpoint, as connoisseurs of trickery.

Instead of rejecting... whatever is archaic, obsolete, or off the beaten path, [the] creative mind integrates it with normal logical processes in what seems a "magic" synthesis, from which the new, the unexpected and the desirable emerge.
Silvano Arieti (1976)[21]

The Future of Warfare. Girls at the front – and they are discussing their usual not very profound subjects. The alarm – the enemy is advancing. Command to the poltergeist girls to concentrate – and under their chairs they stick their wads of chewing gum. A regiment bursts into flames, and the soldiers are torches... Reinforcements are smashed under cliffs that are teleported from the Rocky Mountains. The snatch of Niagara Falls – it pours upon the battlefield. The little poltergeist girls reach for their wads of chewing gum.
Charles Fort (1932)[24]

[The horror movie] is a field in which there is in some sense no original... but only variant; a world in which, therefore, the meaning of the individual example lies outside itself.
Carol Clover (1992)[26]

Rather something akin to the merging of subject and object in meditation occurs. Through the clearing away of narrative context, the possible and impossible aspects of each image compel the viewer to furnish different contexts, from personal memory and free association.

[Subjects were asked to concentrate on a blue vase for 15–30 minutes. They reported the following effects]
a) an increased vividness and richness of the [perception] – "more vivid"; "luminous";
b) animation in the vase, which seemed to move with a life of its own;
c) a marked decrease in self-object distinction, occurring in these subjects who continued longest in the experiment: "I really began to feel... almost as though the vase and I were perhaps merging... It was as though everything was sort of merging...";
d) syncretic thought and a fusing and alteration of normal perceptual modes: "I began to feel this light going back and forth..."; "When the vase changed shape, I felt this in my body..."
A. J. Deikman (1966) [29]

Other kinds of interpretative fusion are encouraged to occur, impelled by a "decrease in self-object mediation" between the viewer and the work. This happens as a natural result of attending to the piece over a certain duration of time, assisted by its various rhythms of repetition. Psychologically, the brain has time to recognise, manifest and absorb the hidden or submerged knowledge that it is only cinematic convention which insists that these elements be read as a fiction of the paranormal at all. In this state of mind, distinctions between levels of reality within the image become elided. The Psi Girl making the pencil spin, the Psi Girl watching the pencil spin, and the imaginary nature of the way the pencil is actually spinning, become equal elements in the "same" consciousness. This becomes clearer if you imagine alternative ways of filming a child "thinking" (or dreaming) about running a spoon up a wall, or spinning a pencil; the dreamed or wished-for action might be shown inside a graphic thought-bubble, as in a cartoon. Hiller's treatment makes visible the cinematic equivalent of the convention of the thought-bubble; ultimately so that it can be read as something else.

[We recognise] how great an influence folk fairy-tales have upon the mental life of our children. In some people a recollection of their favourite fairy-tales takes the place of memories of their own childhood: they have made the fairy-tales into screen-memories.
Sigmund Freud (1913) [30]

Under Hiller's alterations, the "marvellous" images become referents pointing beyond the shared world of fears and fantasies which supplied the conventions for the original movies. They re-compose in the viewer's mind as meta-figurations for a different echelon of mental experience, as if their science-fictional aspect were just a cloak – a "screen-memory", as Freud called it – for things less directly representable. Both installations operate rather like a set of points at a railway junction, directing us towards primary processes of consciousness, which in contemporary culture are often seen as characteristic of childhood, as well as visionary, experience. It is these processes, I suggest, which are both subject and medium in Hiller's art. To discuss them, I will borrow two old words: *thymos* and *techne*. *Thymos* is an ancient term meaning *high* or *daring spirit*, such as characterised the Homeric heroes or Viking *berserkers*. It emanates from the assumption that human nature is inherently daimonic; the word carries the implication of lost or absent self-control. *Thymos* is released when the ego is over-ridden by a flood of passion, capable of filling the world, transforming its owner, and breaking the bounds of nature. In the old Germanic languages, also, *dream* meant "excited consciousness": a disturbance in the head, waking or sleeping, caused by joy or drunkenness, or by another person's murderous desire.[31]

Malignant mists and bursts of fire... flickered red in the vaporous clouds that rose boiling above his head, so fierce was his fury... The hero-halo rose out of his brow... long as a snout... Then, tall and thick, steady and strong, high as the mast of a noble ship, rose up from the dead centre of his skull a straight spout of black blood, darkly and magically smoking...
The Táin (8th C, AD) [32]

So the Celtic hero, Cúchulain, visibly changes under the impetus of his battle-fury; in a manner remarkably similar to that of a two-year-old child in the grip of a tantrum. Of the two works, *Wild Talents* is proportionally more concerned with this dangerous sense of *thymos* in children and adolescents, though elements threaded through *Psi Girls* connote its presence: the gospel clapping and the white noise "collapse."

The second word, *techne* derives from the Greek root for work, weaving, informed play, or artifice of any kind. It too conveys a sense of ego-release, achieved this time through absolute control or focus; the ordinary "magic" of concentration on the task in hand. *Techne* is evoked in *Psi Girls* through the youth of the protagonists, the ordinariness of their props, and particularly their *absorption* in their magical games. This experience of total engagement in play is common to all children: games with train-sets, pencils, cups, or whatever lies to hand, induce absorption in a private imaginary world.[34] Hiller's images recall the child's fluid sense of self, capable of investing any object with life and agency, apprehending no distance between desire, thought and action. Memories of this phantasmagoric infant reality are triggered by the "spoon-games" and animated toy sequences in *Wild Talents*.

Two distinct kinds of ludic wildness – of the mind reaching out to shape the world – are thus given a different balance in each work. Hiller re-sets boundaries and frames her source-materials as fantastical "screen-memories", directing us more towards a sense of *thymos* in *Wild Talents* and more towards *techne* in *Psi Girls* (though some of both are in each).

Analysing Freud's account of the *Traumwerk* (dream-work), the mechanism by which inchoate desire gets attached to figuration and so produces dreams, Lyotard concluded that "*the dream-work does not think*".[37] The modern experiences of *thymos* and *techne* all have at their core a release from, or suspension of, normative consciousness. So too might we consider Hiller's artworks as invoking aspects of consciousness which "do not think"; which have their somatic and occult *umwelt* outside the conventions of language. The "ego-text" is supernaturally expanded or contracted, yet these states are experienced as centres of selfhood, desired ends of consciousness.

In these magical works, often Hiller's starting-point is what we might call the half-conscious mythology of the contemporary collective-fantastic: ecstasy and sleep, memory, science fiction, special effects, childhood play. She collects, selects and orchestrates materials pertaining to this mythology, seeking and releasing its common structures, in order to create analogues for experiences whose existence is eclipsed or marginalised in the dominant fields of explanation. According to Synesius, all states, waking or sleeping, where the ego "roams free" or hovers in suspension, must be understood as equally important habitats for the life of the mind (*intellectus*). *Witness, Dream Screens, Wild Talents* and *Psi Girls* direct our attention to some current locations of such habitats, and to the conventions which frame and govern our awareness of them. Each installation can be understood as a kind of magical Synesian engine, designed to run inside and outside the head. Each is a precise demonstration of how "things which have not a nature capable of existence" are constantly manifested at the interfaces of psyche and desire; each therefore tilts the viewer towards a new consideration of the limits of rational narrative, the moving edge, so to speak, of language-bound experience.

The practice of suture – like the ego's movement in and out of "normal consciousness" – thus emerges in Hiller's art as a creative act; it is at once her subject, object and medium. Engaging with her works, we discover that *thymos* and *techne* can be rooted anywhere, in anybody. Todorov's "hesitation" before the fantastic is reactivated as a portal, less to a literal supernatural realm, than to Gell's permanent occult dimension of consciousness – *the place where I am when I am not happening* – redefined as a shared state of being, marvellous and ordinary at the same time.

...to lose one's way in a city, as one loses one's way in a forest, requires practice... late in life, I learned this art: it fulfilled the dreams whose first traces were the labyrinths on the blotters of my exercise books.
Walter Benjamin (19—) [33]

All kinds of ideas, [of] all degrees of puerility and importance, appear in our minds under the conditions [we] have found to be those of revelation.
James H. Leuba (1925) [35]

The belief that because a thing is not stressed it must be important is not entirely without merit... By the same token it is a prejudice to assume that a thing must be central because it looks marginal. Yet, the supposition that some things which look marginal may be central is one of these judicial reflections that rarely fail to open up new fields of knowledge, because they introduce a change of focus.
Edgar Wind (1968) [36]

In the hollow gulf of the universe how many intermediate places do you think there are, partly obscure and partly luminous, in all of which the soul has habitation, together with this spirit-envelope, changing with it its ideas and morals and life?... the best nurture for us is that we should become active by the force of application, anticipating the onsets of weird and headlong visions, and that the emanation of life should be, as far as possible, once and for all intellectual...
Synesius of Cyrene (d. 412 AD) [38]

51
—

Witness 2000
Artangel at The Chapel,
Golborne Road, London

was in the most beautiful place that I had ever seen, and I felt like I was really there

J'avais une impression de grande tranquillité. Tout d'abord

They told me up

Everything was stunningly beautiful – so vibrant and luminous... and so full of life – yet, life – in ways that one would never

Here are our greatest achievements, truths that people most want

'Mark', he said, 'Soon

Notice more the suggested

The grass was so very green and the trees were more beautiful than I had ever seen...

I went into a tunnel... like the

There was

J'ai eu droit au flashback de toute ma vie passée. On aurait dit des diapositives bombard...

into a bright cloud... it was

...or experience on the physical plane. I was totally and completely immersed in divine Love. It was unconditional love... in the there was

Estuve 12 horas con respiraci

I was

all your troubles, fears and worry will be over

Everything was interconn

the air was a freshness that I cannot explain. I could move from one place to the other in

and it smells like ning evid and awful

vie que j'avais totalement oubliés. J'ai eu l'impression que cela a duré entre 40 minutes

seemed to last ten seconds

una cúpula, una luz blanca pero con un tinte celesti

of a golden

...ink of an eye, and everywhere I went was different but just as beautiful.

... a light is in the distance I'm

...e heure. Ensuite, j'ai eu une impression de grande sérénité, de grande tranquillité. Un peu

que irradiaba rayos de energía.

Light.

...ll of a sudden, I got a rush of love...

...surrounded by the most beautiful living light.

getting closer. . . .

comme si j'étais déconnecté de mes cinq sens, sans aucune perception du monde extérieur.

I cannot describe it... I was awed.

Works Illustrated

Works are listed according to page number. Dimensions are listed in order of height x width x depth. All works collection of the artist unless otherwise stated.

Selected Bibliography

1973 Carla Liss, Lynne Tillman 'Elements of Science Fiction' *Art and Artists* vol. 8, no. 7, October, London

1976 Susan Hiller *Rough Sea* Gardner Centre for the Arts, University of Sussex, Brighton

John Sharkey 'In Pancake Making, It's the Mix that is Important' *Musics* (Actions/performance issue) no. 9, September, London

David Coxhead & Susan Hiller *Dreams: Visions of the Night* Thames & Hudson, London; Editions du Seuil, Paris; Umschau Verlag, Frankfurt, reprinted 1989, 1991, 1993

1977 Caryn Faure-Walker 'In the Beginning was the Word: Susan Hiller's Recent Work' *Artscribe* no. 5, February, London

Richard Cork 'Storm in a Postcard' *Evening Standard* March 17, London

1978 David Elliott, Caryn Faure-Walker *Susan Hiller: Recent Works* (ex. cat.), Museum of Modern Art, Oxford / Kettle's Yard, Cambridge

1979 Susan Hiller *Enquiries/Inquiries* Gardner Centre for the Arts, University of Sussex, Brighton

Tim Guest *Monument* (ex. cat.) A Space, Toronto

1980 Sarah Kent 'Susan Hiller' *The Hayward Annual* (ex. cat.) Hayward Gallery, London

Lisa Tickner '10 Months' *Block* no. 3 London

1982 Roszika Parker 'Dedicated to the Unknown Artists' *Spare Rib Anthology* Penguin Books, Harmondsworth

1983 Susan Hiller *Sisters of Menon* Coracle Press, London

1984 Guy Brett, Roszika Parker, John Roberts *The Muse My Sister: Susan Hiller 1974–84* (ex. cat.) Orchard Gallery, Derry, London

1985 Annette van den Bosch 'Susan Hiller: Resisting Representation' *Artscribe* No. 46 May–July, London

Catherine Kinley (Lacey) 'Susan Hiller: "Belshazzar's Feast"' *Tate New Art / The Artist's View* (monograph series) Tate Gallery, London

1986 Lynne Cooke 'Elan' *The British Art Show* (ex. cat.) British Council, London

Lucy Lippard *Susan Hiller: Out of Bounds* (ex. cat.) Institute of Contemporary Art, London

1987 Sandy Nairne 'Creativity' *State of the Art* Chatto & Windus, London

1988 Gary Indiana 'Wave Theory' *Village Voice* 12 April, New York

Roberta Smith 'Susan Hiller' *New York Times* 15 April, New York

1989 Jean Fisher 'Susan Hiller' *Lifelines / Lebenslinien* (ex. cat.) British Council / Tate Gallery, Liverpool

Peter Schjeldahl 'The Great Unknown' *7 Days* vol.2, no. 2, New York

Susan Butler 'Dream Documents' *WASL Journal* no. 29, London

1990 Jean Fisher *Susan Hiller; The Revenants of Time* (ex. cat.) Matt's Gallery, London/ Mappin Art Gallery, Sheffield / Third Eye Centre, Glasgow

1991 Guy Brett 'Susan Hiller's Shadowland' *Art in America* April, New York

Barbara Einzig 'Within and Against: Susan Hiller's Non-objective Reality' *Arts* October, New York

Susan Hiller, ed. *The Myth of Primitivism* Routledge, London and New York

1992 Susan Hiller 'Hélio Oiticica: Earth, Wind and Fire' *Frieze* Nov/Dec, London

1993 Andrew Renton 'In Conversation' *Talking Art* Institute of Contemporary Art, London

Susan Hiller 'O'Keefe as I See Her' *Frieze* Summer, London

1994   Michael Corris *Susan Hiller* (ex. cat.) Gimpel Fils, London

Michael Archer, interview *Audio Arts Magazine* vol 14, no.1, London

1995   Stuart Morgan, Frances Morris 'Susan Hiller' *Rites of Passage* (ex. cat.) Tate Gallery, London

Stuart Morgan 'Beyond Control' *Frieze*, Summer, London

Susan Hiller *After the Freud Museum* Book Works, reprinted 2000, London

1996   Jean Fisher '*Elan* and other Invocations' *Inside the Visible* (ex. cat.) MIT Press, Boston

Denise Robinson 'Thought Burned Alive: the work of Susan Hiller' *Third Text* no. 37, Winter, London

Guy Brett, Rebecca D. Cochran, Stuart Morgan *Susan Hiller* (ex. cat) Tate Gallery, Liverpool

Barbara Einzig, ed. *Thinking about Art: Conversations with Susan Hiller*
Manchester University Press, London and York

James Clifford 'Immigrant' *Routes: Travel and Translation in the Late 20th Century*
Harvard University Press, Boston

1997   Michael Archer *Art Since 1960* Thames & Hudson, London

1998   Denise Robinson, Stuart Morgan *Wild Talents* (ex. cat.) Foksal Gallery, Warsaw / ICA, Philadelphia

Susan Hiller *Freudsche Objekte* Institut für Buchkunst, Leipzig

Louisa Buck *Moving Targets: A User's Guide to British Art Now* Tate Gallery Publishing, London

Tony Godfrey *Conceptual Art* Phaidon, London

1999   Chris Turner, Matthew Higgs *Psi Girls* (ex. cat.) Tensta Konsthall, Stockholm / Site Gallery, Sheffield

Tim Guest, Richard Grayson, Denise Robinson et al. *Lucid Dreams* (ex. cat.)
Henie Onstad Kunstsenter, Oslo

Susan Hiller, Fiona Bradley, Jean Fisher *Dream Machines* (cat. for ex. curated by Susan Hiller)
South Bank Centre, London

Susan Hiller 'Dream Mapping' *British Journal of Psychotherapy* July, London

Gavin Jantjes, Susan Hiller interview *A Fruitful Incoherence: Dialogues with Artists on Internationalism*
Institute of International Visual Art, London

2000   Susan Hiller, James Lingwood *Witness* (includes cd) Artangel, London

2001   Cecilia Fajardo, Richard Grayson, Denise Robinson *Susan Hiller: Video Installaciones* (ex. cat.)
Fundación Eugenio Mendoza, Caracas

Mary Horlock, Susan Hiller interview *Paletten* July, Stockholm

2002   Ian Hunt 'An Entertainment' *Factor 1991* Foundation for Art & Creative Technology, no. 2, Liverpool

Rachel Withers 'Witness' *(The World May Be) Fantastic* (ex. cat.) Sydney Biennale, Sydney

Anastasia Boudanoque, Oleysha Turkinya 'Susan Hiller in Freud's Dream Museum' *Art & Dreams*
The Freud Museum of Dreams & The British Council, St.Petersburg

Louise Milne, Mette Marcus, Marianne Bech *Susan Hiller: Psi Girls / Witness / Wild Talents /
Dream Screens* (ex. cat.) Museet for Samtidskunst, Roskilde

2003   Jean Fisher 'Susan Hiller: Elan and Other Evocations' *Vampire in the Text: Narratives of
Contemporary Art* Institute of International Visual Arts, London

Charles Esche 'Susan Hiller' in '10 Source Artists' *Cream 3* Phaidon Press, London

2004   Rosemary Betterton 'Susan Hiller Painted Works' *Unframed: Practices & Politics of Women's
Contemporary Painting* ed. Rosemary Betterton, London

Essay Notes

Introduction *James Lingwood*

1 Susan Hiller, 'Art & Anthropology / Anthropology and Art', 1977, published in *Thinking about Art: Conversations with Susan Hiller*, edited and introduced by Barbara Einzig, with a preface by Lucy Lippard, p.19

2 Denise Robinson in this publication, p.102

3 Susan Hiller, *After the Freud Museum*, 1995, unpaginated

Susan Hiller's Painted Works *Rosemary Betterton*

A slightly longer version of this essay appears in Rosemary Betterton (ed.) (2004) *Unframed: Practices and Politics of Women's Contemporary Painting*, London: I.B.Tauris, pp.79–95

1 Hesse's work has long been regarded as a precursor of the concerns of feminist artists in the 1970s, particularly for her feminine practice based on the experience of a sexed body (Lippard,L., *Eva Hesse*, New York University Press, 1976). She was profiled, along with other contemporary American women artists, in *The Feminist Art Journal* co-edited by Cindy Nemser in the early 1970s. Lippard included Hesse in her curated exhibition, *Eccentric Abstraction* in New York in 1966. Lippard also wrote the catalogue essay for Hiller's 1985 exhibition at the Institute of Contemporary Arts, London, which was reprinted as a preface to Barbara Einzig (1996) (ed.) *Thinking About Art: Conversations with Susan Hiller*, Manchester: Manchester University Press.

2 Eva Hesse's diary entry, October 28, 1960, quoted in *Eva Hesse*, New Haven: Yale University Press (1992).

3 Krauss, R. (1994) *The Optical Unconscious*, Cambridge, Mass. & London: MIT Press, pp.19, 24, 313. Krauss draws on the work of Gilles Deleuze and Felix Guattari (1983) *Anti-Oedipus* Minneapolis: University of Minnesota Press, to sustain her argument about the 'body without organs'.

4 Lippard, L. *Eva Hesse*, op. cit., p.56

5 Briony Fer explores the idea of blankness in Hesse's work in Fer (1994). As Norman Bryson put it in a different context, something is 'missing, but what it is can never be named because it is precisely, absence.' (Bryson 1983: 71)

6 Lippard, L., *Eva Hesse*, op. cit., p.192. This is analogous to the claim made by W.J.T. Mitchell that the silencing or repression of language in modernist abstraction was shattered in the mid 1950s by Jasper Johns' *Flags* and *Targets* which marked 'the resurgence of artistic impurity, hybridity and heterogeneity summarised as the "eruption of language into the aesthetic field"' (Mitchell, W.J.T. *Picture Theory*, Chicago: The University of Chicago Press, 1994, p.239).

7 Many of Hiller's earliest works are of this type including 'Cloth books' 1971, '*Sisters of Menon* sewn canvases', 1972, and 'canvas and paper formats', 1974 (Kettle's Yard and Museum of Modern Art 1978: 34).

8 Brett, G, 'The Materials of the Artist', in *Susan Hiller*, Tate Liverpool, 1996, p.16

9 I am using the term 'viewer' rather than 'spectator' to avoid this more distanced form of the gaze: 'looker' would be more accurate, but less grammatical. Norman Bryson argues that 'glance' rather than 'gaze' implies a less authoritarian and more durational kind of viewing, but this does not help with an appropriate noun for the subject position involved (Bryson 1983: 94).

10 Mitchell, W.J.T. (1996) 'What Do Pictures Want?' *October*, 77, summer, pp.71-82

11 Fisher, J. (1994) 'Susan Hiller: *Elan* and other evocations' in C. de Zegher (ed.) *Inside the Visible: an elliptical traverse of 20th century art, in, of and from the feminine*, MIT Press: Cambridge, Mass. & London, p.62

12 Hiller developed an enduring interest in indigenous cultures from her early field research as an anthropologist in Central America in the 1960s.

13 Morgan, S, 'Beyond Control: an interview with Susan Hiller', in *Susan Hiller*, Tate Liverpool, 1996, p.35

14 Ibid.

15 Bois, Y. A. (1986/1992) 'Painting: the Task of Mourning' reprinted in F. Frascina & J. Harris (eds.) *Art in Modern Culture: an Anthology of Critical Texts*, London: Phaidon Press Ltd., p.326

16 *Susan Hiller*, Tate Liverpool, 1996, p.60

17 Lauren Berlant comments on the significance of her own archive on contemporary American life as follows: 'These materials frequently use the silliest, most banal and erratic logic imaginable to describe important things, like what constitutes intimate relations, political personhood and national life.' (Berlant 1997: 12)

18 See Tate Gallery Liverpool (1996) for a fuller account of Hiller's experiments with automatic writing and drawing.

19 Lippard, L. (1986) *Susan Hiller: Out of Bounds*, Institute of Contemporary Art, London, unpaginated

20 These observations are similar to those made by Deborah Cherry in a paper on Zarina Bhimji's installation, *She Loved to Breathe – Pure Silence*, 1987, at the Association of Art Historian's Conference, Liverpool, April 2002. I am grateful for her comments.

21 Hiller, S. (1983) *Sisters of Menon* Coracle Press, London

22 These concerns are evident in the writing on feminist philosophy by Elizabeth Grosz (1994) and Moira Gatens (1996) in Australia, and Iris Marion-Young (1990) and Judith Butler (1993) in the United States.

23 Battersby, C. (1998) *The Phenomenal Woman: Feminist Metaphysics and Patterns of Identity*, Polity Press: Cambridge, pp.38, 57/8

24 Examples of similar practices include the painter, Lee Krasner, who cut up her old drawings and re-made them as collages in the 1950s, and Helen Frankenthaler who let paint flow and

stain un-primed canvas on the floor emphasising the tactili-
ty of the medium. Newman's *Webs (Backlight)*, 1993, use a
process of layering and repetition of marks each of which,
while partially obliterated by another layer of paint, remains
visible underneath.

25 Lippard, L., *Eva Hesse*, op. cit., p.24/5

26 Hesse recorded the strong impression made by her reading
of Simone de Beauvoir's *The Second Sex* (1949/1983) in her
diary. She was aware of the gendered prejudices of her own
time against women artists, but did not take any part in the
emerging women's art movement in New York (Lippard, L.
Eva Hesse, op. cit.). Like Sylvia Plath, Hesse's early death has
given her the aura of tragic, misunderstood genius, rather
than taking part in a sustained tradition of female authorship.

27 Several recent studies have begun to recover the complexi-
ties of art by women in this period, which because of its
timing was not previously 'read' as feminist. See L.C. Jones,
(1993) 'Transgressive Femininity: Art and Gender in the
Sixties and Seventies' in J. Ben Levi, C.Houser and,
L.C. Jones and S.Taylor (eds.) *Abject Art: Repulsion and
Desire in American Art*, New York: Whitney Museum of
American Art, and S. Watling (1998) *Pauline Boty: Pop
Painter* in S.Watling and D. A. Mellor (eds.) *Pauline Boty:
The Only Blonde in the World*, London: Whitford Fine Art
& The Mayor Gallery Ltd.

28 Lippard, L., *Eva Hesse*, op. cit., p.210. As Alison Rowley
explains, the experience of seeing Hesse's latex over rope
works like *Untitled*, 1964, at the Tate Modern in 2003 was
very different from in its original state, the work having
'turned opaque with age, darkened, hardened and begun
to crack', A Rowley (2003) 'not painting, not sculpture':
Review of *Eva Hesse*, Tate Modern, 13 November 02 – 9
March 03, *Textile: the Journal of Cloth and Culture*, 3,
Autumn 2003.

29 Morgan, S, 'Beyond Control: an interview with Susan
Hiller', in *Susan Hiller*, op. cit., p.34

Analysis and Ecstasy *Guy Brett*

1 Susan Hiller, 'I Don't Care What It's Called' (1982), in
Thinking About Art: Conversations with Susan Hiller (ed.
Barbara Einzig), Manchester and New York: Manchester
University Press, 1996, p.46

2 'Looking at New Work: interview with Rozsika Parker'
(1983), ibid., p.56

3 Ibid., p.58

4 Quoted in John Sharkey, 'In Pancake Making, It's the Mix
that is Important', *Musics* (London), no 9, September
1976, p.3

5 Stuart Morgan, 'Beyond Control: an interview with Susan
Hiller', in *Susan Hiller*, Tate Liverpool, 1996, p.35

6 Susan Hiller, 'Notes IV', in *Sisters of Menon*, London:

Coracle Press for Gimpel Fils, 1983

7 Susan Hiller, 'Looking at New Work', *Thinking About Art*,
op. cit., p.51

8 Susan Hiller, 'Thirteen Male Absences: interview with Paul
Buck' (1978), *Thinking About Art*, op. cit., p.136

9 Ibid.

10 Ibid.

11 Ibid.

12 Susan Hiller, 'Looking at New Work', *Thinking About Art*,
op. cit., p.51

13 Susan Hiller, 'Dream Mapping', *New Wilderness Letter*,
no. 10, Winter 1981

14 Walter Benjamin, 'To the Planetarium' (1925–26),
in *One Way Street*, London: New Left Books, 1979, p.103

15 Susan Hiller, 'Looking at New Work', *Thinking About Art*,
op. cit., p.51

16 André Breton, 'The Automatic Message' (1933), reprinted
in *What is Surrealism? Selected Writings of André Breton*
(ed. Franklin Rosemont), London: Pluto Press, 1978, p.105

17 The book of *Sisters of Menon* was published in 750 copies
by Coracle Press for Gimpel Fils, London, and each one
had a different version, or a different segment, of a common cover design: a hand-made field of blots and dots
suggesting a cosmos of a vast or a minuscule scale.

18 Susan Hiller, 'Reflections' (originally the William
Townsend Lecture delivered at the Slade School of Art,
London, 1989), in *Thinking About Art*, op. cit., p.75

19 Susan Hiller, interviewed in *Fuse*, Toronto,
November/December 1981

Wicked Beauty *Ian Hunt*

Originally published in *Factor 1991*, ed. Claire Doherty
(FACT, the Foundation for Art and Creative Technology:
Liverpool, 2002); here printed in shortened form.

1 W.G. Sebald, *The Rings of Saturn* (London: Harvill, 1998),
p. 80; Nietzsche, *The Birth of Tragedy* [1872], (New York:
Doubleday, 1956), p.20

2 'Reflections' in Einzig, B. (ed.), *Thinking About Art:
Conversations with Susan Hiller* (MUP, 1996), p.70

3 Jean Fisher, 'The Revenants of Time', in *Susan Hiller*
(Matt's Gallery, London / Mappin Art Gallery, Sheffield /
Third Eye Centre, Glasgow, 1990), n.p.

4 Copy in Matt's Gallery archive. For technical information

5 From correspondence with Susan Hiller, 2001

6 The gibbet is thus equated with the Christian cross and
the pagan tree. Mummers' plays, which have also been
researched and filmed by the artist, revolve around
St George's defeating of various opponents, Turkish
Knight etc. One of the opponents of St George is, strangely,
Father Christmas, who is in early manifestations an
ambiguous figure not clearly identified on the side of

'good'. See, on this and on Punch and Judy, *The Oxford Companion to the Theatre*.

Before Testimony *Jean Fisher*

1 'It is self-evident that nothing concerning art is self-evident anymore, not its inner life, not it's relation to the world, not even its right to exist.' Theodor W. Adorno. *Aesthetic Theory*, trans. Robert Hullot-Kentor, London: Athlone Press, 1997, p.1

2 Giorgio Agamben, *Remnants of Auschwitz: The Witness and the Archive*, trans. Daniel Heller-Roazen, New York: Zone Books, 2002, p.12

3 Walter Benjamin, 'The Storyteller', in *Illuminations*, trans. Harry Zohn, New York: Schocken Books, 1969, p.89

4 Giorgio Agamben, *Infancy and History: Essays on the Destruction of Experience*, trans. Liz Heron, London and New York: Verso, 1993, pp.14–15

5 Ibid, p.14

6 Giorgio Agamben, *The Man Without Content*, trans. Georgia Albert, California: Stanford University Press, 1999, p.108

7 Elaine Scarry, *The Body in Pain: The Making and Unmaking of the World*, New York and Oxford: Oxford University Press, 1985, pp.33–35

8 During the late 1960s he conducted a series of experiments where he left a tape-recorder running in an empty soundproofed room, claiming that the resultant amplified recordings were the voices of historical figures who had their own transmission station.

9 Agamben, *Remnants of Auschwitz*, op. cit., p.39

10 Catherine Clément, *Syncope: The Philosophy of Rapture*, trans. Sally O'Driscoll and Deirdre M. Mahoney, Minneapolis and London: Minnesota University Press, 1994, pp.235–242

"...scarce stains the dust..." *Denise Robinson*

This text is an extensively revised version of my text on Susan Hiller's retrospective at Tate Liverpool, 1996, 'Thought Burned Alive' publ, *Third Text*, no 37, Winter 1996–1997, p.37

1 The title '...scarce stains the dust...' comes from Samuel Beckett, 'For to End Yet Again' 1975, in *For To End Yet Again*, John Calder, London, 1999, p.13

2 Giorgio Agamben, *The Man Without Content*, Stanford University Press, 1994, p.106. Re Benjamin's work on Baudelaire, Agamben comments:" the poet who had to face the dissolution of the authority of tradition in the new industrial society...to invent a new authority, by making the very untransmissibility of culture a new value by putting shock at the centre."

3 Susan Hiller, Part 1, editor's introduction, *The Myth of Primitivism*, (ed) Susan Hiller, Routledge, London and New York, 1991, p.11

4 Susan Hiller, *From the Freud Museum*, Book Works, London, 1995

5 Susan Hiller, *From the Freud Museum*, Afterword (unpaginated), ibid.

6 Giorgio Agamben, 'The Melancholy Angel' in *The Man Without Content*, Stanford University Press, 1994, p.104

7 Giorgio Agamben 'Walter Benjamin and the Demonic: Happiness and Historical Redemption', *Potentialities*, pp.148

8 Susan Hiller, *After the Freud Museum*, Book Works, London, 1995

9 Jacques Lacan 'Touche and Automaton', *The Four Fundamental Concepts of Psychoanalysis*, (ed.) Jacques Alain Miller, London, The Hogarth Press and Institute of Psychoanalysis, 1977, pp.53

10 Walter Benjamin, 'Edward Fuchs, Collector and Historian', *One Way Street and Other Writings*, trans. Edmund Jephcott, Kingsley Shorter, Verso, London & New York, 1979, p.351

11 In discussion with Susan Hiller during her exhibition at Tate Liverpool, 1996

12 K. Reinhard, *The Freudian Thing, Construction and the Archaeological Metaphor*, (ed.) Stephen Barker, State University of New York Press, Albany, New York, 1996, p.60

13 Conversation with the artist, February 2004

14 See the framed texts of the automatic writing experiments, in many of her works, or Hiller's use of Raudive's voices in *Elan* or more oblique references in the later video installations such as *Wild Talents* or *Psi Girls*.

15 A.Weiss, 'Stein's Stein, a Tale From The Aphoristic Theatre' in *Experimental Sound and Radio*, MIT Press, 2001, p.95

16 Discussion with Susan Hiller in February 2004

17 For a discussion of Hiller's video installations see my text 'Wild Talents' in the catalogue for the exhibition, *Wild Talents*, publ. Galeria Foksal, Warsaw, and the Institute of Contemporary Art, University of Pennsylvania, Philadelphia, 1997 – also exhibited at Experimental Art Foundation, Adelaide, Australia, 1998

18 Samuel Beckett, 'For to End Yet Again' ibid., p.13

Anamorphosis of the Gaze *Stella Santacatterina*

Edited version of an essay first published in *Portfolio* no 36, December 2002

1 Roger Caillois, *Méduse et Cie*, Paris, 1960

2 Maurice Blanchot, *Lo Spazio Letterario*, 1967

On the Side of the Angels *Louise Milne*

First published in *Susan Hiller* exhibition catalogue, Museet for Samtidskunst, Roskilde, 2002

1 *The Essays and Hymns of Synesius of Cyrene, including the Address to the Emperor Arcadius and the Political Speeches*, trans. w. intro and notes, A. Fitzgerald (London, 1930), p.355

2 Quoted in E. Smedley, W. Cooke Taylor, H. Thompson, eds., *The Occult Sciences* (London-Glasgow, 1855), p.91

3 *Flying Saucers*, trans. R.F.C. Hull (London, 1959), pp.40–41

4 *The Cult of Pan in Ancient Greece*, trans. K. Atlass and J. Redfield (Chicago, 1988), p.91

5 Longus, 2.25.3–4; Loeb ed., trans. G. Thornley, rev., J. M. Edmonds. I am indebted to Borgeaud (97, 110) for this quotation.

6 All quotations from the testimonies are taken from the associated book/CD, Susan Hiller, *Witness* (London, 2000).

7 *The Fantastic* (1970), trans. R. Howard (1973), p.25

8 Roger Caillois, *Au Cœur du Fantastique* (Paris, 1966), quoted in Todorov, p.26

9 *Oratio* XLVIII, 31-35, trans. Georg Misch, *A History of Auto-biography in the West* (Cambridge, MA, 1951), pp.210–211

10 G. V. Ksenofontov, *Legendi i rasskazy o shamanakh u yakutov, buryat i tungusov*, trans. Adolf Friedrich and Georg Buddruss, as *Schamanengeschichten aus Sibirien* (Munich, 1955); cf. M. Eliade, *Shamanism: Archaic Techniques of Ecstasy* (Princeton, NJ., 1964), pp.36–7

11 *Otia imperialia* I.2, c.85; I.3, c. 95; cf. Joseph Hansen, *Zauberwahn, Inquisition und Hexenprozess im Mittelalter* (Munich, 1900), pp.139–140

12 In English, the double sense of *witness* as testifier to a divine manifestation and as testifier to a crime goes back c. 950 AD; according to the *Oxford English Dictionary*. *Witness* could also be used to mean (visionary) wisdom.

13 Susan Hiller, *Witness* (London, 2000), p.73

14 Alfred Gell, 'Understanding the Occult', *Radical Philosophy* 9 (Winter, 1974), p.20

15 Gell, pp.20–21

16 'Metaphor of the Eye', in G. Bataille, *The Story of the Eye*, trans. 1979, Penguin, pp.120–1. I have taken the liberty of changing the word 'Eye' to 'the work' in this quotation.

17 *Precepts of the Painter* (MS. 2038 Bib. Nat. 22v.), in *The Notebooks of Leonardo da Vinci*, ed. & trans. E. MacCurdy (1939; New York, 1955), pp.873–874

18 *www.diacenter.org/hiller/biblio.html*; trans. from Henry Corbin, Visionary Dream in Islamic Spirituality, in G. E. von Grunebaum and R. Caillois, eds., *The Dream in Human Societies* (Berkeley, 1966).

19 *On the Necessity of Violation*, reprinted in M. R. Sandford, ed., *Happenings and Other Acts* (London, 1995), pp.272–3

20 Celia Green and Charles McCreery, *Apparitions* (1975; Oxford, 1989), p.7

21 *Creativity, the Magic Synthesis* (New York, 1976); cf. discussion in A. Geels, 'Mystical Experience and the Emergence of Creativity', in N. G. Holm, ed., *Religious Ecstasy* (Stockholm, 1982), pp.27–62

22 Charles Fort (1874–1932) devoted his life to researching and writing about contemporary strange and inexplicable phenomena. For a hypertext version of Fort's *Wild Talents* (in progress), see www.resologist.net/talent

23 Ossowiecki disciplined an inner cacophany and used it to help amongst others, archaeologists and the Polish Resistance in Warsaw. Incidentally, in pre-industrial Europe, locating lost items was a common form of work for traditional village psychics. An ongoing investigation of his life and career has acted as an 'objective correlative' in Hiller's recent work, informing the conception of *Witness* also.

24 Quoted from *Wild Talents*, 1042, www.anomalist.com/fort

25 Quoted by Chris Turner in *Psi Girls* (Sheffield, 2000), p.7

26 *Men, Women, and Chainsaws* (London, 1992), p.11

27 The smallest units of myth; cf. Claude Lévi-Strauss, 'The Structural Study of Myth', ch XI in *Structural Anthropology* I (1963; London, 1973).

28 Though the literature on *Wild Talents* and *Psi Girls* to date usually describes the filmic sources as 'popular cinema', in fact, the list includes as many art cinema directors (Andrei Tarkovsky, Stanley Kubrick, Peter Brook and Brian De Palma et al), as lesser-known 'genre' or popular directors.

29 A. J. Deikman, 'Deautomatization and the mystic experience' *Psychiatry* 29 (1966), pp.324–338

30 'The Occurrence in Dreams of Material from Fairy-tales', in *Zeitschrift*, I (1913); trans. J. Strachey (1925); *Collected Papers* IV (London, 1948), pp.236–43

31 For examples, see E. C. Ehrensperger, 'Dream Words in Old and Middle English', *PMLA* 46(1) (March, 1931), pp.80–89

32 *The Táin*, trans. T. Kinsella (Oxford, 1969), pp.150–153; cf. C. O'Rahilly, ed., *Táin*, Recension I (1976), p.187

33 Quoted in Susan Sontag, *Under the Sign of Saturn* (London, 1996), p.112

34 On the complexity of the relations between play and the imagination, see Brian Sutton-Smith, *The Ambiguity of Play* (Cambridge, Mass., 1997), pp.127–172

35 *The Psychology of Religious Mysticism* (1925; London, 1972), p.243

36 *Pagan Mysteries in the Renaissance* (rev. ed., New York-London, 1968), p.203

37 Jean-François Lyotard, 'The Dream-Work Does Not Think', trans. M. Lydon, in A. Benjamin ed., *The Lyotard Reader* (Oxford, 1989), pp.19–55

38 As for n.1; pp.340–1

This essay is dedicated to the memory of my grandmother, Agnes Campbell Brown (1901–2002), who taught me the meaning of *thymos*.
I would like to thank Susan Hiller for her very generous assistance in the preparation of this work.

Credits and Sources

BALTIC

BALTIC Centre for Contemporary Art
May 1 – July 18 2004
Director: Stephen Snoddy
South Shore Road, Gateshead, NE8 3BA, United Kingdom
Tel.: +44 (0)191 478 1810   Fax: +44 (0)191 478 1922
Email: info@balticmill.com   www.balticmill.com

MUSEUSERRALVES
MUSEU DE ARTE CONTEMPORÂNEA

Museu de Arte Contemporânea de Serralves
October 15 2004 – January 9 2005
Director: João Fernandes   Deputy Director: Ulrich Loock
Rua D. João de Castro, 210, 4150 – 417 Porto, Portugal

Kunsthalle Basel

Kunsthalle Basel
January 30 – March 27 2005
Director: Adam Szymczyk
Steinenberg 7, Basel 4051, Switzerland

ISBN 1-903655-19-6 (English edition)
ISBN 972-739-129-x (Portuguese / English edition)
ISBN 3-033-00095-9 (German / English edition)

Edited by James Lingwood
Designed by Mark Diaper, Eggers + Diaper, Berlin
Photography by: Alan Cruickshank, pp.97, 124–129; David Coxhead, pp.13, 31; Prudence Cuming, pp.50, 51; Colin Davison, pp.92–93, 95; courtesy of Delfina Gallery, London, pp.132–137; Jean Fisher, p.77; courtesy of Galeria Foksal, Warsaw, pp.118, 123; courtesy of Gagosian Gallery, New York, pp.130–131; courtesy of RHA Gallagher Gallery, Dublin, pp.56–57; Dirk Pauwels © S.M.A.K., pp.84–85; Chris Swayne, pp.14, 28, 29; Roger Sinek, pp.23, 87–90 ; Parisa Taghizadeh, pp.150–155; Rodney Todd-White & Son, courtesy Gimpel Fils, London, pp.24–25; Stephen White, pp.52, 53, 112–115; Edward Woodman, pp.32, 40–47, 62, 67–75, 106–111

Distribution (English edition)
Cornerhouse Publications Ltd.,
70 Oxford Street, Manchester, M1 5NH, United Kingdom
Email: publications@cornerhouse.org
Tel.: +44 (0) 161 200 1503   Fax: + 44 (0) 161 200 1504

D.A.P. Distributed Art Publishers, Inc.,
155 Sixth Avenue, 2nd Floor, New York, NY 10013, USA
Tel.: (212) 627 1999   Fax: (212) 627 9484

With acknowledgements to the following, for material used in the exhibition.

From India to the Planet Mars
Bate, Jean *The First Three Months* 1985
Bond, F. Bligh *The Gates of Remembrance* 1917, 1930
Breton, André *Le Message Automatique* 1933
    (Mme. Smead, "Max")
Douglas, Nik *Book of Matan* 1977 ("a young man")
Flournoy, Th. *From India to the Planet Mars* 1898
    (Hélène Smith)
Harper, George M. *The Making of Yeats' 'A Vision'* 1987
    (George Yeats)
Hiller, Susan *Sisters of Menon* 1972
Holzer, Hans *Elvis Presley Speaks* 1978 (Dorothy Sherry)
Muhl, Dr. Anita *Automatic Writing: an Approach to the Unconscious* 1963 (anon. analysands)
Oliver, Fred *Dweller on Two Planets* 1974
    ("Phylos the Thebetan")
Rodari, Florian *Shadows of a Hand* 1998 (Victor Hugo)
Spare, Austin Osmond & Carter, Frederick "Automatic Drawing" *Form* vol. 1, no. 1, April 1916
Volunteer art students 1996 –7
Toksvig, S. compiler *Swan on a Black Sea* 1986
    (Cummins, Geraldine)

Psi Girls
Brian De Palma *The Fury* 1978 20th Century Fox
Andrew Fleming *The Craft* 1996 Columbia
Danny De Vito *Matilda* 1996 TriStar Pictures
Mark Lester *Firestarter* 1984 Universal
Andrei Tarkowsky *Stalker* 1979 Mosfilm (Russia)
The music is edited from a field recording of the gospel choir of St.George's Cathedral, Charlotte, North Carolina

Wild Talents
Roger Christian *Nostradamus* 1993 Vereinigte
Ken Russell *Mindbender* 1996 Buena Vista
Stanley Kubrick *The Shining* 1980 Warner Bros.
Tobe Hooper *Poltergeist* 1982 MGM
Emir Kusturica *Time of the Gypsies* 1989 Forum (Sarajevo)
Carl Schultz *The Seventh Sign* 1988 Columbia Tristar
John Hough *Escape to Witch Mountain* 1974 Buena Vista
Peter Brook *Meetings with Remarkable Men* 1978 Fox
Frank Oz *The Indian in the Cupboard* 1995 Paramount
David Lean *Blithe Spirit* 1945 J. Arthur Rank
Brian De Palma *Carrie* 1976 MGM
John Hough *The Watcher in the Wood* 1982 Buena Vista
Mark Lester *Firestarter* 1984 Universal
Andrei Tarkowsky *Stalker* 1979 Mosfilm (Russia)
Brian De Palma *The Fury* 1978 20th Century Fox
Lewis Gilbert *Haunted* 1995 Lumière/Zootrope
Jorge Montesi *Visitors of the Night* 1997 Marquee